The Ugly Canadian
The Rise and Fall of a Caring Society

The Ugly Canadian

The Rise and Fall of a Caring Society

BARBARA MURPHY

Cover design by Terry Gallagher/Doowah Design Inc.
Printed and bound in Canada

Published with the assistance of the Manitoba Arts Council and
The Canada Council for the Arts.

Canadian Cataloguing in Publication Data

Murphy, Barbara
        The Ugly Canadian: the rise and fall of a caring society

ISBN 1-896239-45-5

        1. Canada—History. I. Title.

FC164.M87 1999   971   C99-900153-1
F1034.2.M87 1999

Acknowledgements

Tracing the shifts in public support for Canadian social legislation would not have been possible without the extensive collection of newspapers, parliamentary debates, and sessional papers held by the National Library of Canada and the National Archives of Canada. I am grateful for the courtesy and excellent service provided by the staff of both.

I am also greatly indebted to the research of Malcolm Taylor whose *Health Insurance and Canadian Public Policy* provided valuable chronology and background for the chapter on the development of national health care.

Finally, I am especially grateful for the contribution of Debbie Lyon whose editing skills made the content of the chapters that follow more accurate and, at the same time, more comprehensive.

Table of Contents

Preface

The end of the century is one of those few times when we like to look back and try to discern some national trends over the long haul. At other times, in a world moving too fast, we're inclined to believe that time spent reviewing the past is unproductive. Canadians, in particular, are not noted for their interest in their own history.

If the end of the century is the right time for history I'm reluctant to let the opportunity pass. The growth of social conscience in Canada (and its subsequent decline) has been one of the major trends over the last hundred years. It has often been overshadowed by more tangible trends which lend themselves to measurement and more easily meet the criteria of hard evidence and proof.

These are not only the criteria of journalism (where the media indulge in retrospective analysis at certain milestones) but of the social sciences. Students learn early that the intangible is not held in high repute. I can offer a brief example. A few years ago when an emergency arose I was asked to teach an undergraduate social work course called *The Political Economy of Social Welfare*. (Since I'd never given the course before and was actually a trespasser in the academic world, I have a vivid memory of preparation hours far outnumbering actual class hours.) The course covered the development of social legislation in Canada and it was intended to help students understand the political and economic context of that development. The emphasis was on political economy with, of course, the usual hoops students are put through in applying a number of theories which they may never use again throughout their entire lives.

Over the semester I was struck by the sense of powerlessness I was imparting to students in using a political economy approach. Never once were the words "social conscience" used. Instead we found a cause for everything in the political and economic structure of society, the nature of which, it was implied, was beyond our control as ordinary citizens.

In these pages I hope to correct this imbalance and restore a feeling of power and responsibility. Structural causes are only part of the story of Canada's social legislation. By exercising our franchise over the years we made governments at all levels aware of what we considered acceptable. As ordinary Canadians, we were responsible for the development of some humane and generous policies. By the same token, if we're distressed at what we've become at the end of the century — less caring, less attractive — we have only ourselves to blame.

Barbara Murphy
January, 1999

CHAPTER 1

Risks in Helping the Poor

In Canada we hold fast to a conviction that we have become a caring society, a "kinder, gentler" society (to use the catchwords of the 1990s) than we were in earlier times. But this is a rather remarkable delusion. If we could measure in some way how we feel about our fellow Canadians, especially those less fortunate than ourselves, we would find we care as little today as we did a hundred years ago. It's true we took a run at compassion, even generosity, during the twentieth century. Following the shock of the Great Depression we spent over 40 years caring about each other. It became acceptable to be concerned, to contribute part of our incomes to looking after those with none. We pointed proudly to our social policies *vis-à-vis* those of the United States and guarded them fiercely even as late as the 1980s when free trade was negotiated. Where did all that caring go? We take pride in our toughness now, not our generous social policies. We warn the poor and the sick to keep their heads up; they've had their innings. The years of compassion are over. Today we're playing hardball.

Tough public attitudes in the 1990s are reminiscent of those in the early years of the century when Canada's industrial sector was relatively new. In 1901 over 65 percent of Canadians still lived in rural areas and 40 percent of the labour force still worked in agriculture. We lagged behind both Great Britain and the U.S. in industrialization. But we had moved sufficiently away from total reliance on a staples economy to begin to experience industrial fallout — stark living conditions for workers even when they were employed, low standards of safety in factories resulting in disabilities and loss of income, exploitation of child labour, widespread poverty in periods of unemployment, and the fate of poverty or death for the elderly who could no longer work.

Despite these consequences of industrialization, a nation predominantly rural believed strongly in self-sufficiency. After all, many still remembered their parents clearing the eastern and central provinces of the country with the sweat of their own labour, and in the West the whole cycle was just beginning. So in response to the growing demands of workers in the industrial sector for a better life, the answer was usually no. The average Canadian felt no collective responsibility for the lot of the poor and wanted no government action that indicated there might be such a responsibility. Helping people out would reduce their incentive to work — or so went the prevailing philosophy.

Such sentiments are not unfamiliar today. If the extent of Canada's social conscience has come full circle through the century, there is a danger that over time history may not record the intervening years, the years that truly *were* kinder and gentler. Future generations may never know what used to set us apart, especially in North America. In the interests of accuracy the chapters that follow tell the story of how Canadians grew into caring citizens before losing it all. It was not governments but Canadians who were responsible for the development of social programs, just as Canadians are now responsible for their decline. Throughout the century our values changed and governments responded.

For some it may require a giant leap of faith to assume that broad public opinion has a role to play in influencing government. Social scientists have written at great length about the process through which government responds to public opinion. Many argue that there is no role for the masses, or at best that it is a passive role. Instead, the argument goes, an elite group of individuals influences government action, a small powerful group made up of people who hold the highest positions in the country's economic and political institutions. Still others contend that government decides and acts in response to pressure from one or more interest groups. Women, seniors, labour, farmers, Native peoples, ethnic groups, environmentalists, big business, small business, banks — all have the ear of government at one time or another. In fact, government is seen as an umpire presiding over the power struggle among these special interests.

There is, of course, some validity in these theories of how government links with the public. Powerful arguments may be made that a pressure group or an elite has left its mark on individual pieces of legislation. Besides responding to such pressures, governments have also on occasion taken the initiative in stimulating public interest in particular policies. Indeed, so essential is public support to the success of these initiatives that governments have used their power to manipulate public opinion to meet their short-term goals. But a trend that covers a century of social policy is another matter. Although the general public may be passive between elections, its influence in the long run is of a different kind. Voters not associated with powerful groups or not easily influenced by government efforts to shape public opinion can clearly put governments in or out of power. In doing so, they set the outer limits of acceptable public policy over the long term. In other words, despite some erosion of democratic principles, government still responds to the "will of the people" in the twentieth century.

Tracking social legislation is a way of showing changes in public values and it will be used as the general framework for this review. A more direct way of showing changes would be the recording of values and attitudes actually expressed by Canadians over the years, an imperfect science at best. In the first half of the century the polling of attitudes was not yet well developed. But on the premise that the media was the voice and ear of the public as it is now, an expression of public opinion from 1900 to 1950 can be found in contemporary newspapers at each period of new legislation. News stories and editorials record the sluggish growth of social conscience up until World War II and into the early postwar period. In later years public opinion polls became available. They reached a broader cross-section of Canadians and showed how general was the growing acceptance of responsibility for the poor and the sick during the next quarter-century before harsh attitudes took over again.

•••

In the first years of the twentieth century Canada consisted of seven provinces and a vast territory north and west of Manitoba as far as the border of British Columbia. The national government was still preoccupied with prairie settlement which had started with the building of the Canadian Pacific Railway. To this end, more railways were planned and many were already under construction. Transcontinental railways and prairie settlement were, of course, important elements in support of Canada's economic development. It was the economy and its needs that drove most actions taken by Parliament. In addition to the larger and larger wheat crops coming out of the West (doubling, in fact, between 1899 and 1901), manufacturing in the East had grown by 82 percent over the previous 20 years. Territorial expansion and economic growth, however, were accompanied by serious unemployment in the large urban centres of Toronto, Montreal, Winnipeg, and Vancouver, despite the speeches of members of the Senate who proclaimed that "we are now in our days of sunshine and industrial prosperity." With Canada's rapid development, they maintained, opportunities existed for everyone to earn decent incomes.

Although economic recessions had started to appear long before the beginning of the twentieth century, social legislation targeting the poor and the unemployed was almost non-existent in the first decade. This was true at the federal level, but to a lesser extent at the provincial. Most provinces had already passed factory acts by 1908; British Columbia had passed a Workmen's Compensation Act. A similar bill was introduced a few years later in Alberta, although it was stalled in the Legislature when angry workers learned, among other things, that they were required to fall from a height of 40 feet before they could claim compensation. But these provincial acts were the extent of social legislation in place in Canada during the first decade. In the midst of the federal government's preoccupation with economic growth and national pride, Robert Pringle, Conservative member for Stormont, rose in the House of Commons on February 20, 1907, and proposed a national old age pension program. Described by the *Ottawa Citizen* as "an able debater," Pringle was a lawyer in his fifties who lived in Cornwall, Ontario, home of one of the largest woollen mills in the country. For the greater part of the afternoon he described to the House the plight of the aged deserving poor in Canada and the pension programs in place in other countries. Because he believed a workingman with his $300-a-year average earnings could not lay up money for old age, Pringle pressed for a non-contributory pension. This was the model already established in New Zealand, Australia, Denmark, France, and Italy, and it was being considered in the British Parliament. At the conclusion of Pringle's address, the prime minister was on his feet immediately. Immaculately dressed, carrying his authority gracefully, Sir Wilfrid Laurier spoke amicably and with respect. The subject of Mr. Pringle's resolution was, of course, "one which must in an eminent degree command the attention and sympathy of all those who have any humanitarian feelings in their heart." It was a subject, however, full of difficulties. The granting of a pension to a recipient who had not contributed "a single farthing" would be unacceptable. On the other hand, a system of state annuities, in which the workingman could purchase an annuity over his lifetime at a low price, would encourage working people to be thrifty.

> But to ask purely and simply that there should be an old age pension whether a man has been thrifty or the reverse, whether he has been sober or not, whether he has been a good citizen or a bad citizen, is going further than I would be disposed to go.

Advised by the prime minister to leave the matter stand for another session to allow for public discussion, Pringle withdrew his motion.

It is difficult to know with certainty if Laurier's position on old age pensions reflected public opinion. Newspapers in all regions of the country (including Saskatchewan and Alberta, carved out of the Northwest Territories only two years earlier) carried an account of the debate in the Commons, but only the *Globe* in Toronto went beyond the basic news report. In an editorial on March 1 the *Globe* saw the problem as one of inadequate wages. If Parliament would concern itself with seeing that every productive worker received the value of his services, the editorial argued testily, there would be no demand for old age pensions. Despite these words of support for the workingman, the *Globe* went on to claim that old age pensions were not only too expensive, but were too inclined to discourage thrift on the part of working people. Legislators were warned to be cautious.

For the most part Pringle's resolution and the prime minister's comments were received with polite indifference by the Canadian public. The *Montreal Gazette* called the debate "a pleasant academic discussion." Within a week the subject of old age pensions had moved to the Senate where Sir Richard Cartwright, minister of trade and commerce, responded with a new solution. An imposing man with large whiskers and small eyeglasses, an eloquent speaker without the prime minister's conciliatory manner, Cartwright laid out a detailed plan on February 28 for a system of state annuities remarkably similar to that proposed by the prime minister. In the plan a workingman would voluntarily place part of his earnings over his lifetime into the safekeeping of the government and would receive an annuity when he was too old to work. It was clear to anyone who knew anything about the situation of the industrial working class that the plan was based on a complete misconception of the workingman's earnings and way of life.

But if this was the testing ground, the proposal came through with flying colours. It was hailed by various speakers as a worthwhile solution for the aged poor, allowing those "in the vigour and prime of their life to make some provision for their old age." In distinguishing government annuities from old age pensions, however, members of the Senate provided, perhaps unwittingly, some evidence of prevailing attitudes about the poor. Cartwright spoke at length on the subject:

> I am free to admit that I have always regarded the case of honest, industrious men, who have for many years led a life of toil and at the end of their lives find themselves...thrown on the charity of their neighbours or their relatives, as pre-eminently deserving the compassion and consideration of everybody, and if it were possible to confine the question of old age pensions to that particular class, I do not know that I...would object to introducing some such measure.

The problem was that in a great many cases the industrious workingman may have "dissolute" companions who would be extravagant with their earnings if they no longer had to worry about their old age. Cartwright dismissed the claim of inadequate wages — there was no question of Canadian workingmen living from hand-to-mouth as they did in older countries. Given Canada's prosperity, there was very little risk of any hard-working able-bodied man not being able to make adequate provision for his old age.

In the debate that followed, the charge that an old age pension system would contribute to laziness was made more than once. "We should rather encourage people to provide for themselves," said one member. "If they fail to make provision for their old age and cannot look to their friends for help, in nine out of every ten counties in the country there are poorhouses." And if they had made good use of their opportunities earlier, he scolded, none of them would find it necessary to end up in the poorhouse.

The frightening prospect of extravagance came up again and again. Old age pensions would be fatal to thrift and, therefore, "would strike a fatal blow at one of the fundamental elements in the development of character." There would also be repercussions for the nation: "....[I]f that habit of extravagance is once cultivated and grows, the wage-earners and breadwinners may find themselves late in years penniless and dependent, and, as a consequence, the credit and honour of the country will suffer and the status of Canada will be affected accordingly."

There were arguments against dependence and in favour of self-reliance — the gift of a pension in a great many cases would debase and demoralize the worker. The duty of the government, members of the Senate were reminded, was "to help men to help themselves and not to pander to folly and improvidence."

As the man responsible for laying the state annuities plan before the Senate, Cartwright concluded the debate eloquently:

> ....[W]e have the lessons of history to teach us — the Roman people never lost their liberty till the people were fed by the state. I have no sympathy with the class of maudlin philanthrophists who would reward the idle sensualist at the expense of the honest, frugal and industrious. And if hon. gentlemen think that this is too hard a saying I may remind them that there was once a great saint...who has left his views on the subject on record in the memorable saying, 'If a man will not work neither let him eat.'

Having used the Senate as a forum for his annuities proposal, Cartwright perhaps hoped to influence broad public opinion. But if he waited to hear what Canadians across the country thought of his proposal, he waited in vain. News stories were carried in the *Halifax Chronicle* and the *Manitoba Free Press* without editorial comment, but the annuities plan failed to make the pages of the newspapers in the other Maritime provinces or in B.C., Alberta, or Saskatchewan. In Central Canada there was a glimmer of interest. A *Globe* editorial on March 2 praised the plan for providing a solution to poverty in old age "without any dangerous or deteriorating socialistic departure." Moreover, the *Globe* stated, the plan included nothing that could "pauperize" workingmen or deprive them of the incentive to individual effort or thrift. The *Montreal Gazette* on the same day noted: "Sir Richard Cartwright's plan for old age pensions for workingmen is hardly what the advanced socialists who make much noise in Canada just now had anticipated." According to the *Gazette*, however, his annuities plan was as far as public opinion was likely to go.

Robert Pringle, member of Parliament for Stormont, dutifully waited, as advised by the prime minister, to allow time for public discussion. He would surely have been disappointed at the sudden disinterest of the public and the press in the months that followed his and Cartwright's strongly divergent proposals. Still, in February of the following year, he again placed a resolution before the House of Commons. This time he proposed that a select committee be appointed to consider solutions. He took issue with Cartwright's arguments that pensions would discourage thrift among working people and even took issue with the prime minister who, according to a recent press report, had claimed an old age pension plan would have all the paupers and criminals of the United States coming to Canada to qualify for the 20 years' residence. But this time Pringle asked only for the appointment of a committee and, after a short debate, the House approved.

The resolution for a select committee was reported in most Canadian newspapers from coast to coast. The estimated cost of $40 million for old age pensions quoted by the finance minister was given prominence in some of the coverage but, in the main, there was little reaction. The *Montreal Gazette* on February 5 commented that Pringle's pension plan would entail large tax contributions from "the provident" in Canada while the benefits would be divided between "the unfortunate, who are subjects of pity, and the improvident, who are not." It was as if the press were waiting for the other shoe to fall. A plan of government annuities (rather than old age pensions) was about to be announced, or so said the speech from the throne at the beginning of the session.

A month later, on March 10, the Government Annuities bill was introduced in the House. The objective, according to the government, was to provide small or moderate annuities at the lowest possible price and with the greatest possible security. But there was another objective. It was clear the bill was Cartwright's plan of a year ago, dusted off and spruced up, and it was intended to lay to rest any demand for old age pensions. Pringle had been outflanked. One member attempted to bring out the story behind the bill:

> Mr. Foster: Will the Minister of Finance give to the House any information as to the pressure put upon the government for this legislation? Were there any petitions or demands made for it?
> Mr. Fielding: I am not aware of any. Certainly there was no pressure.

By now the press appeared bored with the subject. In most newspapers the Government Annuities bill was buried in a report on increased subsidies for Canadian dry docks. After the bill was given third reading and sent to the Senate, Pringle was told that, due to the pressure of House business, it would be impossible for the select committee on old age pensions to meet again in the current session. His old age pensions proposal was dead and newspapers across the country failed to report it.

Can the argument be made that the opposition to old age pensions was really not a reflection of social values? Could it be argued that the image of the workingman as extravagant and inclined to laziness was planted and nurtured to cover up the real reason for opposition, an anxiety about the high cost of a program of such magnitude? The facts suggest otherwise. The finance minister, who had caught the public's attention in February with his prediction that old age pensions would add an enormous charge to the obligations of the country, presented his budget in March. A surplus of $19 million was projected, the largest in the history of the dominion.

And we can look outside the old age pension issue for evidence of less-than-benevolent social attitudes at the turn of the century. Most care and relief for the poor was still given through church and charitable societies. These societies were in the process of streamlining their activities to prevent ingenious individuals among the poor going from one charity to another to get more than one hand-out.

In an article in the *Manitoba Free Press* on March 14, 1908, a charity worker extolled the virtues of modern philanthropy. He proudly reported that in the new century the chaos of former charity works had been replaced by scientific investigation. Classification of the poor was important: "Our poor will fall naturally into two classes, those who ought to be helped and those who ought to be punished." In the first class were widows with families of young children, and those reduced to poverty through illness, accident, or lack of employment (the unemployed particularly were singled out as "social misfits"). In the second class of poor were the professional beggar and vagrant, requiring stern and prompt treatment:

> The habitual vagrant in addition to having no abode, no support and no work, has no intention of working. This intention to remain idle should be met with severe repressive measures, such as imprisonment at actual hard labor in jail, workhouse or penitentiary, but better still by commitment to a compulsory labor colony with indeterminate sentence.

It has to be conceded that every charity worker can have a bad day. In this case the worker was not only contemptuous of the beggar, but he also maintained that the dependence of the *deserving* poor was due to a number of character defects, among which were intemperance, incompetence, immorality in its various forms, and shiftlessness.

In fairness, it should be noted that the worker also acknowledged that causes of dependency could be partly social. He pointed out that "intelligent workers and students in the field of charitable effort" no longer attributed all poverty to deficiencies in the individual — they believed the true cause was to be found in insufficient incomes. It was clear from his own solutions, however, that these theories were not yet widespread.

Nor can we attribute harsh sentiments exclusively to prairie cities. On March 11 of the same year, the *Vancouver Province*, commenting on a bill about unemployment being debated in the British House of Commons (which House, incidentally, the *Province* followed in their pages diligently while they usually gave short shrift to the business of the Canadian House of Commons), warned:

> Giving alms to the unemployed is merely a palliative. It can easily degenerate into a means of fostering pauperism, as [a member of the British cabinet] himself recently proved by joining a line of men applying for charity and receiving his soup and bread unchallenged.

In the end the Government Annuities Act of 1908 made little dent on poverty. A 1915 review in the *Political Science Quarterly* showed that labourers accounted for only four percent of all applicants for annuities under the new program (the majority of applicants were people of middle income). A range of choices open to the poor for the spending of their discretionary income was a fiction of people who had never experienced poverty. Indeed, discretionary income itself was a fiction. If it was true the twentieth century belonged to Canada, Canadians were clearly not ready yet to take ownership. The poor would have to wait for the development of a social conscience, and in the first decade of the century they were well-advised not to hold their breath.

CHAPTER 2

The Beginning of Compassion

It was clear Canadians in the first decade of the century had as little interest in a program of state annuities as they had in the poor. And in the urban centres the poor were increasingly in evidence. Without the collection of census information on income, the extent of poverty is difficult to determine today but several studies confirm that it was considerable.[1] Members of the House of Commons and the Senate, caught up in Canada's growing prosperity, were inclined to deny that poverty existed and consistently gave low estimates of the number of poor. On the other hand, Canadians in closer touch with real life watched the extent of poverty grow each year along with the growth of industry. Whatever the true number, it increased dramatically in the 20 months immediately before World War I when the economy suffered another recession and thousands found themselves out of work. When war came many idle workers went into the army along with those leaving their jobs, but unemployment continued to be a problem well into 1915.

Almost three-quarters of a million Canadians went to war during the next four years; more than 60,000 gave their lives; three times as many were wounded. Though these sacrifices were made to support the "mother country" and allies abroad rather than fellow Canadians, they were remarkable examples of caring. And if Canadians on this occasion showed themselves capable of caring, it is also sobering to consider who exactly was showing themselves capable. By and large it was ordinary workingmen who sacrificed their lives, the very people who would surely become dissolute and indolent, it was generally believed, if Canadian society mistakenly lent them a helping hand.

That these attitudes were so widespread in Canada may seem incompatible with the level of consciousness and pride reached by the working class at the beginning of the twentieth century. It was pride, but it was also a kind of morality. In a society with greater attachments to formal religion than today, the influence of sanctions originating in religious belief was still strong. For workingmen every bit as much as for their employers, the work ethic and "God helps those who help themselves" were part of a moral outlook that promoted and secured a kind of personal discipline. This discipline translated into the glorification of an honest day's work.

The truth was that harsh attitudes about the workingman were historically British, and in the early 1900s almost 60 percent of Canada's population was of British origin. (It is of passing interest that Sir Wilfrid Laurier, who was of French descent for at least eight generations, saw fit to remind his colleagues of the potential for "slovenliness and want of diligence" in workers during the old age pension debate.) Because of the origin of these harsh attitudes, it may be worthwhile to recollect their historical basis in Britain.

A great deal has been written about the English Poor Law, a system of providing for the poor that was later adopted in British North America in only two provinces, Nova Scotia and New Brunswick. Briefly, it stipulated that the poor were the responsibility of municipal authorities, a responsibility they shouldered in England for over 300 years. Connected closely with labour statutes, the poor law required local parishes to provide work or relief for their own poor and unemployed. From the standpoint of the poor, relief meant being housed in a local workhouse where they were required to work for their keep. This came to be known as indoor relief insofar as it meant the poor could either take the food, shelter and compulsory work or remain outside and starve. "Poor rates" were levied on local farmers to cover the costs and, with the expected grumbling about periodic rate increases in times of high unemployment, the workhouse and indoor relief were used for over 200 years.

When change came, it was not the poor who brought it about but the ratepayers. Experiments near the end of the eighteenth century, especially in parishes where the cost of a workhouse was prohibitive, stopped the practice of indoor relief and allowed relief to be given without requiring the poor to enter the workhouse. In the new arrangement the unemployed were usually housed on a rotation basis with local farmers who provided work. This was outdoor relief, a not-altogether unsatisfactory solution but one that came under severe criticism from Poor Law Commissioners in the early nineteenth century.

During their review of outdoor relief practices, the commissioners heard a litany of complaints from those responsible for supervising the poor. Among them, and with great consistency, was the complaint that giving cash assistance to workingmen (rather than requiring them to work in the workhouse) had resulted in a lazy, shiftless labour force with no incentive to work.

Despite later research showing no loss of worker productivity during the years of outdoor relief, the conclusions reached by the Poor Law Commissioners became accepted truths in Britain. Outdoor relief was immediately abolished and the poor were in for seven decades of harsh treatment, which diminished only slightly with newer reforms at the turn of the century.

But these new reforms were not yet part of general knowledge in Canada, and public resistance to helping the poor remained firm. During World War I the first tiny cracks began to appear. Nothing had really changed. The credo of self-sufficiency had a stronghold and the belief that any kind of assistance to the poor would provide a disincentive to work was deep-seated. There were two groups, however, for whom the incentive to work had very little application. Injured workers thrown into poverty as a result of factory accidents made up one group — with their capacity to work temporarily or permanently gone, there was no need to talk about incentive. The same could be said about the second group, mothers who found themselves and their children in poverty as a result of the death of the family breadwinner. It was unreasonable to expect a widow to be wage-earner and homemaker at the same time. Concerns about her incentive to work, therefore, were academic. Some of the first pieces of twentieth-century social legislation in Canada were aimed at these two groups.

A third group was also in line for social reform. Except for those out of the labour force for good reason, the expectation of society was a fair day's work remunerated with a fair wage. But among those giving a fair day's work was an exploited group of women who were paid less than a living wage, a peculiar circumstance justified on the grounds that they were not family breadwinners. Social legislation introduced near the end of the war made an attempt to solve this problem.

•••

The issue of compensation to injured workers seemed at first to belong to the area of labour relations. There appeared to be no reason for public concern or action. Provincial factory acts had in most cases tackled the problem of safety in the workplace before the beginning of the century. If the odd accident should occur after safety regulations were in place, it should be a matter between the employer and the worker. There was, in fact, legislation in most provinces that laid out the ground rules for both parties in damage claims through the courts, including a range of acceptable circumstances under which employers would *not* be found liable.

But the reality was anything but the occurrence of the "odd accident." Factories were becoming more and more mechanized, making life more dangerous for workers. Outside of the factories railroad work took the largest toll. In 1907 one out of every 136 trainmen was killed and one out of every 23 injured. Scarcely a day went by without a newspaper report of a serious factory or railway accident. A sample of headlines appearing in a single month in 1907 in the *Halifax Chronicle, Toronto Globe*, and *Edmonton Journal* tells the story:

Injured as a Result of Blasting Accident

Killed at Leamington—Explosion Blows Part of Elmer Townsend's Head Off

Sad Death at Arnprior—Chas. Worm Killed in McLachlin's Lumber Yards—Crushed Between Pole and Freight Car—Leaves Wife and Child

Buried Under Coal Slide—Frank Mahaffey of Sault Ste. Marie May be Fatally Injured

Charge Exploded and Two Coal Miners Injured

Killed in Collision—Two Men Lose Their Lives in Nova Scotia—CPR Train Crashes Into Night Express

James Maynes Killed—Struck by a Flying Board in Saw Mill

Two Men Killed—Dynamite Explosion on the Transcontinental North of Dryden

Five Firemen Injured—Serious Fire in London Planing Mill

One Killed, Many Hurt—Special Freight Smashes Into a Pulp Train

A Brakeman Killed—Run Down by Train at Hamilton Junction

The existing employers' liability acts soon came under attack. Based on the principle that negligence on the part of the employer was the sole ground for compensation, they required the workman to provide proof that he had not *to any degree* contributed to the accident through his own negligence. Even in cases of defective machinery, the courts assumed that the worker took upon himself the risks of the job when he was hired. It is not surprising that under the old legislation awards were granted in very few cases.

Pressure for an improved workmen's compensation system began in the early part of the century. After a series of labour delegations persistently presented their position to the Alberta government, a new act in 1908 recognized the principle that the employer was liable not only for his own negligence, but also for that of any of his workmen. Quebec, acting on the recommendations of a royal commission on labour accidents, followed suit the following year, as did Manitoba and Nova Scotia.

But the principle that the employer was responsible for all accidents met with strong opposition in other parts of Canada and it was the first hurdle to be overcome before the introduction of modern workmen's compensation legislation in every province. Despite a U.S. investigation showing that only a small portion of factory accidents in that country was the fault of the worker, Canadian industry still went along with the conventional wisdom that

95 percent of accidents could be traced to worker carelessness. The Canadian Manufacturers' Association (CMA) commented in its periodical *Industrial Canada*:

> Accidents result chiefly from three causes: carelessness of employees, unguarded machinery, and defective equipment. The first is the principal cause, as all manufacturers know.

If the large majority of accidents was caused by workers, why should industry enter into a no-fault system and assume total liability? A Canadian Lumbermen's Association official called the new legislation "tyrannous" and "unjust," adding:

> ....[I]t provides that compensation must be paid without regard to how the injury was brought about; it puts the employer and employee in bitter antagonism to each other...therefore the bill is vicious in its effects; it is the most glaring example of class legislation with which any community was ever threatened.

It will mean, said another lumber executive, the closing of factories and a reduction in employment. Whatever kind of bill was put through, it was certain the employer would come off second best.

The issue was finally settled in 1912 when the CMA on behalf of industrial employers began to see advantages in taking compensation claims out of the courts. Litigation was sometimes bitter, made for poor labour relations (and poor public relations), and resulted in costly and unpredictable awards. A system of liability without fault could provide automatic compensation without litigation. It would also have the benefit of fixed costs for employers. Reversing its former position, the CMA finally accepted the principle that the employer was responsible for all accidents in his workplace.

But it was not enough. Workers demanded that industry also accept the principle that the risk of accidents was part of doing business and that industry alone should pay the cost of insuring against those risks. Canadian employers bitterly opposed this proposal, contending that premiums should be split between employers and employees. In a speech reported in the *Toronto Globe,* the president of the Boards of Trade of Ontario asked:

> Is Ontario ripe for such drastic legislation?...Have the vast areas and climatic conditions and the still struggling position of many industries in Ontario been taken fully into consideration?

A plaintive letter from a manufacturer to the editor of the *Globe* outlined the depressed conditions of the woollen industry in Canada and went on to complain:

> When one hears men speak of adding the cost of workmen's compensation to the high charges which already exist and the difficulties under which we labor it makes one feel that all our efforts are to be set aside and that these men do not understand the true condition of affairs.

In the end, on the issue of who should pay, the Meredith Commission inquiring into workmen's compensation in Ontario recommended in 1913 against contributions from employees and set the pattern for legislation in Ontario, Nova Scotia, British Columbia, Alberta, New Brunswick, and Manitoba over the next seven years. These workmen's compensation acts, from 1914 on, recognized the collective liability of industry for factory accidents and required employers to assume all costs without employee contribution.

Something significant was happening. Royal commissions in Quebec, Manitoba, and British Columbia had been appointed to find a method of compensating injured workers that would transfer the responsibility for accidents from the worker to the employer. An Ontario commission of inquiry had been asked to find a method that would give the worker automatic compensation rather than "throwing him upon public charity" while he undertook a lengthy and usually unsuccessful lawsuit. In recommending a method, the Ontario commission also decided employers should pay the whole cost. These actions and the subsequent legislation passed in six provinces were important steps taken by provincial governments in support of the workingman. They gave the first indication that public attitudes toward the poor were softening ever so little.

•••

During the second decade of the century a social reform introduced in one province of Canada spread within a few years across the other provinces. Also typically Canadian was the tendency of each reform to follow on the heels of new legislation in Britain. From the speeches introducing each new act in the various provincial legislatures, one could easily conjure up the image of progressive politicians scanning the pages of Britain's parliamentary Hansard in search of solutions for making life more bearable for the workingman in Canada. But this was far from the case. Governments were pushed into action, and the point at which they yielded to pressure depended on their assessment of public concern about the poor. The pressure came sometimes from labour, still in its early years of organization, and often from labour in alliance with social reform groups.

The alliance of labour and social reform groups in Canada played a major role in the progress, albeit modest, of social legislation in the first quarter of the century. The Canadian social reform movement was part of a broader movement originating in Britain. By the 1890s it had found its way to both the U.S. and Canada where it developed principally under the proactive work of clergymen of various denominations responding to the whole array of urban and industrial problems. The next 25 years were exciting and rewarding ones for the movement.

The alliance with labour was a natural one to attack industrial problems. It began at the turn of the century when social reformers and labour groups took on the common goal of securing a weekly day of rest for working people. Their combined forces were successful in pressing the federal government to pass the Lord's Day Act in 1907 making commercial activities on the sabbath illegal. But this was just the beginning. Their victory led to the creation of a joint council whose broad mandate was the whole range of urban and industrial problems, but whose narrower focus for the next eight to 10 years was the prohibition of liquor. They were joined in this struggle by temperance groups across the country.

At a 1914 congress sponsored by the council (by that time called the Social Service Council of Canada), over 200 participants declared themselves in favour of prohibition, old age pensions, pensions for needy mothers, extension of the franchise to women, better conditions for Indians, and a royal commission to deal with the unemployed. Resolutions demanding legislative action, among them workmen's compensation and the protection of female employees in factories, were passed and forwarded to provincial and federal governments. This was a group with a winning combination of purpose, energy, and moral outrage.

Prime Minister Robert Borden spoke briefly to the large gathering of the congress in Ottawa. But there was an even larger world outside and significantly the prime minister cautioned the audience of progressive social reformers not to expect legislation in advance of public opinion. In the prime minister's jurisdiction, the warning was probably justified. But public opinion was catching up with reformers in some areas of the country, and provincial legislatures were feeling the pressure.

After workmen's compensation, widows' pensions demanded their attention. Originating in the United States rather than Britain, widows' pensions were the exception to the typical social reform pattern. By 1916 legislation providing regular monthly allowances to widows was in place in 23 American states. Pressure on provincial governments to follow the lead of the American reforms came from women's groups supported, as we have seen in the 1914 congress resolutions, by the labour/reform alliance. All groups were aware their proposal had a special significance — it was not to be a program based on the insurance principle (like workmen's compensation) but a program of government allowances, the first venture into public welfare on both sides of the border.

The so-called mothers' pension movement in the U.S. had not been free of problems, according to a study by American researcher Roy Lubove. The original focus of the movement was on children, as it was later in Canada. By the turn of the century public concern had been growing about their placement in institutions, a solution normally used by charities to help lessen the load of the widow suddenly without income. Institutional care, according to the new field of child guidance, was detrimental to the child's development. It was routine, impersonal, and incompatible with progressive child care principles which held that each child needed to develop as an individual. Even the poorest home provided a better environment. The mothers' pension movement spread across the U.S. spearheaded by women's groups who forced a turn-around in social work thinking. To state legislatures they repeatedly made their point: "A child should not be removed from the home for reasons of poverty alone." The obvious solution was to attack the problem of the mother's poverty. This was one case, and the *only* case, where a family might be better served if the parent received an allowance to stay home.

At first the issue broke down into two clear sides. Traditional opponents of any form of cash hand-out (still known as outdoor relief) made no distinction for the widow. All financial assistance, they argued, led to laziness, shiftlessness, and, most certainly, intemperance. These were the ingredients of the dreaded condition known as pauperism. Leaving the child in an institution was preferable to such a sorry state of affairs. The mother must go to work to fulfill her role as a contributing member of society.

On the other hand, those who wanted to return children to their own homes were not in favour of placing them with an absent mother. It was generally believed the children of working mothers were responsible for most juvenile delinquency, a growing phenomenon in urban centres. The mother's place was in the home — with a pension.

But the movement ran into an unexpected stumbling block when the issue became three-sided. Private charity organizations in the U.S. joined the battle with a solution that clearly served their own interests. In their view, children should stay in their own homes while their widowed mothers supported them with food-and-clothing relief from private charity. With private relief there was no need for public financial assistance and the accompanying risks. How could a regular cash allowance with no supervision by social work professionals ensure that the widow would adhere to personal behaviour and lifestyle appropriate for the "deserving" poor? In New York, one of the earliest states to consider mothers' pensions, the opposition of private charities held up legislation for over four years.

In Canada private charity organizations were an obstacle in

some provinces and not in others. They gave full support in Manitoba, the first province to enact legislation, and this in part accounted for the early success in that province. (In Ontario and B.C., where private charities gave strong resistance, legislation was held up for four more years.)

The story of the efforts of Manitoba women's groups to secure widows' pensions demonstrates how well they learned from the lessons of the American campaign. In Manitoba the initiative began in 1914 when a committee of the Local Council of Women in Winnipeg launched and funded an experiment to provide monthly allowances to four widows, each with four small children, for almost a year. The risks of giving outdoor relief were well-known; the experiment was intended to determine if they had any foundation. A year later the committee reported back to the council that the experiment was a success. The widows and their families had been helped "without any pauperizing effects." If legislators dug in their heels and argued that a hand-out would have terrible consequences for the mother and her children, the council now had an answer.

The next step was an alliance with the city's Social Welfare Association made up of local charities similar to those who had opposed widows' pensions in the U.S. This proved to be a happy alliance. The two groups spent six months collecting comprehensive information and statistics on the subject and early in 1916 they presented their findings to members of the Legislature and the press.

The *Manitoba Free Press* gave their work high praise and prominent coverage. An editorial commented:

> The evidence is overwhelming that as things are there is a distinct economic and social loss involved in permitting widows to struggle against impossible odds to bring up their families...Obviously the problem must be faced in Manitoba.

This was a remarkable endorsement from the province's major newspaper.

With the combination of a trial run, scientific study, and appropriate alliances, the Local Council of Women had pushed the widows' pension issue onto the public agenda in less than two years.

At this point a master stroke of timing pushed the issue the final distance. Following a public scandal involving high-level corruption,[2] the government of Manitoba had been forced to resign and the opposition, after a strong election campaign on social reform issues, formed a new government which held 42 out of 49 seats. At times over the next months it appeared the new government couldn't pass bills quickly enough. Two major reforms were the culmination of years of hard work by women: prohibition legislation (in response to pressure from the temperance movement in which women played a large role) and legislation granting women's suffrage, the first in Canada.

It was a heady time for women in Manitoba. This was the way the *Free Press* described the scene in the Legislature the evening the women's suffrage bill was passed:

> When the third reading had been duly and formally given the ladies who thronged the galleries, the men who were also wedged into the galleries, and the members on the floor of the house stood up while the rich soprano of hundreds of female throats sang 'O Canada'. After the singing of the anthem the ladies, with much fervor, took up the rollicking strain of 'They're Jolly Good Fellows' in compliment to the members of the house...

Two days later a delegation from the alliance of the Local Council of Women and the Social Welfare Association placed their case for widows' pensions before the cabinet. To the members of the cabinet the names and the faces of the women pressing for action were not unfamiliar. The same women had been active in the suffrage and temperance movements, and very little stood in their way. Within five weeks the legislation was passed.

Over the next four years similar acts were passed in Saskatchewan, Alberta, Ontario, and British Columbia. Mothers' pensions (called mothers' allowances in some provinces) were the first public welfare programs in Canada. Means-tested, they maintained the distinction of deserving vs. undeserving poor that characterized assistance given by private charities. But there were important differences. Not only was the new form of assistance publicly funded, it consisted of cash payments for the first time, an indication that recipients were considered responsible enough to purchase their own goods and services.

Private charities that opposed and delayed legislation in Ontario and B.C. continued to find fault for many years after, their arguments always the same — public assistance was outdoor relief, and outdoor relief was certain to destroy personal effort and independence. The problem was not poverty, in their view, but personal inadequacy which could only be improved with regular supervision by professional social workers. It was clear from the enactment of Canada's first public assistance program in five provinces that the general public was less reluctant than private charities to give up old attitudes toward the poor.

•••

The public was clearly ready for mothers' pensions. But another goal of the combined forces of women, labour, and social reformers had not yet gained public approval when the first mothers' pensions were introduced — the first minimum wage legislation for women workers would take another two years.

Earlier in the century the issue of low wages for women factory workers had failed to attract a great deal of attention. Only the women themselves considered it a problem. They were relatively new as factory workers, becoming a cheap source of labour (along with children) when industry introduced mass production techniques in the last decades of the nineteenth century. Between 1901 and 1911 the number of Canadian women working in manufacturing grew from approximately 70,500 to 97,000, an increase of 37 percent, while the number of male workers grew by only 20 percent. Concentrated in the garment and textile industries and having little bargaining power, women and children received less than subsistence wages for reasons that were not a secret. "In the textile and cotton trade," said one manufacturer in *Industrial Canada*, "it is impossible to conduct a manufacturing concern and compete with Europe unless you employ child labour."

Someone had to be exploited in the interest of keeping industry competitive. Even as late as 1914 a B.C. royal commission on labour conditions refused to recommend a minimum wage for women and girls on the grounds it would destroy B.C. industries in competition with industries in Eastern Canada or in other countries not saddled with similar legislation. Resistance finally began to give way near the end of the war. Larger industries, where women tended not to be employed in any great number, threw in their support for a minimum wage in order to put an end to the competitive undercutting of wages. Small industries, where women were concentrated, simply lacked the political clout to have their way. Manitoba brought in minimum wage legislation for women and girls in 1918. B.C. followed in the same year. By 1920 Quebec, Saskatchewan, Nova Scotia, and Ontario had also enacted minimum wage acts.

The significance of the new legislation was its reflection of changing public attitudes. A living wage was now considered a minimum — a wage "adequate to supply the necessary cost of living to employees and to maintain them in health," stated the Manitoba bill. Still, though there had been enough change in public opinion to encourage governments to go ahead with legislation, the transformation was not quite complete. Some public reaction showed as much sympathy for employers of low-wage workers as for the exploited workers themselves. Even the progressive publication *Canadian Forum* had reservations about some of the legislative successes achieved by social reform groups. Referring to minimum wage legislation, the *Forum* commented:

> ....[E]very new demand upon the employer makes it more difficult for the small man to carry on, and places additional burdens on the back of the primary producer...do we want to squeeze out the small employer, and how much can the primary producer stand?

In fact, for just these reasons, minimum wage legislation made no significant contribution to lessening poverty in the years that followed, even after it was extended to men. The concern that small employers might be forced out of business by higher wage costs carried more weight than the goal of meeting the requirements for an adequate living. As a result the minimum wage remained below that level for the rest of the century.

CHAPTER 3

Old Age Pensions:
Concession to a Third Party

For the first 20 years of the century Canada's political system was
essentially a two-party system.[3] Preoccupied with railway building,
tariffs, and subsidies, the House of Commons at times took on the
aura of an annual meeting of shareholders. In this setting the appearance of a third party could only mean that some Canadians
were preoccupied with other issues. To debate those issues was sometimes enlightening; to have to act on them was inconvenient. Not
surprisingly, the system of two parties was favoured by Liberals and
Conservatives alike.

Aside from their opposing views on tariffs, the two parties had
a great deal in common. In the development of policies, public
opinion was held in as much respect by one party as the other.
There was also little to distinguish between them in their willing-
ness to act when it seemed prudent to go along with public opinion rather than the wishes of powerful interests in the country. Out
of these few moments of anguished decision-making were born
the first social programs. It was a Conservative member of Parliament in 1907 and 1908 who proposed old age pensions, and it was
a Liberal government that turned the proposal down. Early workmen's compensation acts were brought in by Conservatives in B.C.
and Manitoba, and by the Liberals in Alberta. Liberals enacted mothers' allowance legislation in Saskatchewan and a Minimum Wage
Act in Quebec.

During this period of provincial activity each party in turn took office at the federal level with little to show in the way of social legislation. Four years after Robert Pringle's motion for a committee had been quietly sidetracked, the issue of old age pensions was not quite dead, but it was certainly bedridden. In the interim not a single member of Parliament had asked the whereabouts of the committee. Outside the House labour organizations continued their pressure, gaining very little coverage in or support from Canadian newspapers. Watching the old age pension issue as it made its halting way through to the 1920s was like watching a game of lawn croquet. No sooner did a proposal get through one hoop, sometimes even two hoops as in 1912-13, than a great whack from the mallet of a more skilful opponent would send it hurtling back to the starting post.

This erratic progress was partly due to strongly divergent views of where public opinion stood on the issue. When a further committee on pensions was approved in 1912, Finance Minister Sir Thomas White, one of the first speakers, cautioned that there was no public agitation about old age pensions, a fact he hoped the new committee would take into consideration. Two years later the committee's report was ready but never presented, another victim of government sleight-of-hand. Asked in the House for the report's findings, the committee chairman complained:

> I am not now making a report as chairman of the committee. I am not authorized to do so…

Another member of the committee seemed to attribute the demise of the report to the finance minister. Hadn't he commented two years earlier about the lack of public agitation? If this was the reason the report was being shelved, it was surely based on a faulty assessment of the situation. The committee member argued:

> At the present time there is a ripened and matured public opinion in this country from the Atlantic to the Pacific on the question of old age pensions. I think there can be no doubt of that.

Another speaker had the opposite view:

> ...I will venture to submit that any member of this House who has gone into the question from the standpoint of his own constituency must admit that Canada is not prepared today by any public sentiment for old age pensions.

And that view was challenged by still another speaker who held that there had been "a great development of public opinion in the last few years..."

But the minister of finance stuck to his position. Speaking for the government, he contended that legislation at the present time was premature and he laid to rest the issue of public opinion:

> While it is true that many people in Canada would be advantaged by and are favourably disposed to an old age pension scheme, my observation is that the great majority have hardly given the matter a thought.

He moved for adjournment of the debate, and old age pensions once again were knocked back into oblivion.

The debate was reported in most Canadian newspapers. The absence of editorial comment in all but a few, however, simply reflected the lack of consensus shown in the House. The *Toronto Star* commented:

> The Minister of Finance regards the discussion of old-age pensions as premature. Is that certain? Canada is a young country, but men grow old in Canada as well as in Europe, and the shadow of unemployment and want has already darkened the new world.

The *Ottawa Citizen* took the other side, contending that the government had been wise to turn down the pension resolution. An editorial stated:

> In a land where production is free, where the land is not held by privileged monopoly, old age pensions should be unnecessary.

It was five years before the pension issue surfaced again. World War I had intervened and, though legislation was passed for soldiers' pensions, a national pension system remained on the shelf. At the end of the war labour problems flared up in all sections of the country, prompting the federal government in the spring of 1919 to appoint a Royal Commission on Industrial Relations which might better have been named the Royal Commission on Industrial Unrest. Among the remedies recommended by the fast-working commission (two months!) was early legislation for a system of state insurance against unemployment, sickness, and old age. A follow-up National Industrial Conference in the fall involved industrialists and labour representatives in a final review of the commission's recommendations.

In every region of Canada front-page newspaper coverage of the conference was an indication of the importance attached to finding solutions to the current industrial unrest. British Columbia, hard hit by strikes, was typical. At the outset a *Vancouver Province* editorial, noting that the country was waiting for results from the gathering, commented: "The majority of people wish justice to be done by peaceful and judicious methods and not by industrial war." The *Province* continued to provide moral support during the ups and downs of the five-day proceedings — when reports came back of sharp conflicts of opinion among delegates ("If it were an industrial love-feast it would be a useless gathering...") and when progress at times seemed slow ("It is not uncommon for a parliament to discuss matters for a week without arriving at even one decision.").

By the end of the industrial conference many of the royal commission's recommendations had been endorsed, among them state insurance against unemployment, sickness, and old age. Canada's older worker could finally envision a pension becoming a reality in what was left of his lifetime.

But still no action was taken. Two years later there was every reason to be optimistic again when the throne speech of the new Liberal government included a commitment to investigate the issue of old age pensions. Despite high praise from the House and the press for including it, the government had to be prodded several times over the next two years about the promised investigation. Each time the response grew more vague.

Finally in 1924 a committee to investigate the issue material-ized. Clearly more enthusiastic about old age pensions than the government was, the committee completed its work in six short weeks and presented the shape and substance of a pension system, including details of eligibility and federal-provincial cost-sharing. But once more government inertia set in. Informal negotiations with the provinces dragged on for a year, and the last session of Parliament before the general election closed without the appear-ance of a pension bill.

It would be an understatement to comment that the govern-ment's caution and secrecy were frustrating to those pushing for pension legislation. Over the 18 years, from the first motion in 1907, members asking for government action had been from al-most every part of Canada, from Ontario (1907-8 and 1912), Nova Scotia (1912 and 1914), Cape Breton (1914), Saskatchewan (1921), Quebec (1922), Manitoba (1923), and Alberta (1924). Liberal and Conservative governments in turn had held them off. It would take someone with a special kind of political clout to overcome the resistance.

When the clout was finally wielded it came from a most un-likely source, a new party in the House — one of two non-tradi-tional parties gaining seats in 1921. But to understand how this particular party came to be in the right place at the right time, an explanation is needed for the appearance of new alternatives to challenge Canada's traditional two-party system.

After the war Canadian farmers who had for years pressed pro-vincial and federal legislatures for agrarian reforms became increas-ingly frustrated with the neglect of their interests. In Ontario, an-gered by the sudden postwar drop in the price of farm produce, they formed their own political party and won the 1919 provincial election. In Alberta farmers rolled existing organizations into a new political party and became the provincial government in 1921. In the same year a new federal party, the Progressives, was created when a small group of farmer representatives in the House sepa-rated themselves from the Liberals. In the general election that fol-lowed they took 65 seats.

At the same time new labour political parties were developing as rapidly as farmers' parties. Labour parties were formed in the prairie provinces, British Columbia, and Ontario. It seemed inevitable that a federal labour party would grow out of all this activity, and in 1921 two Labour members won seats in Parliament. Canada's traditional party system was, to say the least, shaken up by these events.

Active in organizing the new farmer and labour parties, especially in the western provinces, were members of the reform movement who had been prominent in the agitation for provincial social legislation over the previous five years. Though reformers had achieved most of their legislative success while working with labour groups, they soon learned that farmers would organize only for their own interests. Despite the obvious benefits of a stronger party if farmers and industrial workers joined forces, farmers were not interested in an alliance with labour. Among other things, rural attitudes taken during the Winnipeg General Strike of 1919 were not easily discarded. Separately, then, the two new parties went to the House of Commons.

One of the Labour members, J.S. Woodsworth, had been a force in all three movements — social reform, labour, and agrarian. His story is of special interest in following the development of social legislation through the first part of the century. In addition to his role during the 1920s, he was destined for an even more important role in the 1930s.

Woodsworth was a former Methodist minister who had worked among the poor in the missions of north Winnipeg in his early career. Struck by the social injustice of urban slums, he spent the next 10 years looking for solutions to the problems facing working people. A leading social reformer, he became actively associated with labour organizations which he believed held the key to social reform, and he played a conciliation role in several industrial disputes. Convinced that the route to social justice was through the formation of a working-class political party, he resigned from the Methodist Church in 1918 to be free to work toward this goal.

While employed as a longshoreman in Vancouver, Woodsworth helped organize a B.C. labour party and made use of his considerable writing experience by contributing articles to the labour paper. It was his writing skill, with its fire and commitment on behalf of workers, that would create a problem for him within less than two months. On a trip to Winnipeg he became actively involved in the general strike, writing and making speeches on behalf of the strikers. He subsequently was arrested and jailed for seditious libel, a charge that was finally dropped eight months later.

It is likely the outcome of the Winnipeg General Strike (the arrest of 10 strike leaders, the armed charge of the mounted police on the strikers) strengthened the movement toward working-class political parties. Four labour representatives were elected to the provincial Legislature in 1920, including three strike leaders who were still in jail. In the following year, running in Winnipeg Centre, Woodsworth was elected to the House of Commons.

Space now had to be made in the House for two new parties. Over the next four years the 65 farmer representatives who made up the federal Progressive Party struggled with their new political role, not always in harmony with each other, leaving themselves vulnerable to co-optation by the new Liberal prime minister, William Lyon Mackenzie King. Many returned to the Liberal fold by the 1925 election and only 25 went to the House as Progressives.

The Labour group with its membership of two had an easier time with internal unity. This was almost assured from the beginning when William Irvine of Calgary, who had run as a Labour-Progressive, rose in the House in the first session and made the introductions. "I wish to state that the honourable member for Centre Winnipeg is the leader of the Labour group," he said, "and I am the group." As J.S. Woodsworth rose to his feet, it was hard to imagine a greater physical contrast than the contrast between this new member and the prime minister who would try to win his support in the House. Woodsworth, with his small frame, appeared almost frail. His trimmed beard also contributed to the look of a disciplined man. Mackenzie King, on the other hand, was already starting to acquire the roundness of face and body that would become familiar to Canadians over the next 20 years. There were other differences, however, more substantial than physical appearance. Woodsworth and his fellow Labour member resisted the prime minister's wooing through four sessions of Parliament and they retained their numbers (still two) in the 1925 election.

But that election was disastrous for the Liberals who, with a weak minority government, became dependent not only on the support of the Progressives, but especially of the two Labour members, Woodsworth and A. A. Heaps (the election had cost Irvine his seat). As it turned out, this new "balance of power" role for Labour would be short-lived, but the tiny, yet suddenly powerful party seized its brief opportunity.

Woodsworth and Heaps may have even realized they held the balance of power before the prime minister did, though this is doubtful. Whichever the case, the election was barely over when they wrote to King asking whether he intended to introduce in the new session provision for the unemployed and old age pensions. The prime minister replied promptly, committing the government to action on both issues. But his reply was only part of a strategy to gain Labour support. According to Grace MacInnis (Woodsworth's daughter and later his biographer), the prime minister met privately with both Woodsworth and Heaps and, without success, offered each of them in turn a cabinet post.

The exchange of correspondence between King and the Labour group took place in January. In February a bill for old age pensions was presented in the House. (The prime minister also made good his promise to help the unemployed by sharing the cost of emergency relief with the provinces and municipalities.) The parliamentary rumour mill was grinding effectively, however, and the reason for the sudden appearance of the pension bill after it had failed to earn mention in the most recent throne speech was well-known.

Looking back on a month of new legislation, a Nova Scotia member asked:

> ...I believe this House has a right to know what was promised with respect to old age pensions. What was promised by Mr. King to the Labour members as an amendment to the Criminal Code of Canada? What was promised by the Prime Minister to be brought down as amendments to the Naturalization Act and the Immigration Act, and other assistance they were demanding for the cause of labour?

A member from B.C. called the presentation of the bill "another indication of political expediency." And another member went further, claiming the prime minister had bargained in bad faith:

> The government expect and hope that the Senate will throw this bill out because it is more or less a controversial piece of legislation. I venture to say there will be — what? fifty members sitting behind the Prime Minister, fifty members of his own party who would rather this legislation was not before the House.

Another member agreed with this assessment of the situation and contended the bill was drafted to hoodwink members of the House, a statement that was challenged:

> Mr. Brown: Does the honourable member think the labour men are so easily fooled?
>
> Mr. Nicholson: …[W]hether they are fooled or not fooled, this bill is designed to fool them and designed to fool every other working man who is depending on it.

It was clear the addition of third parties to the parliamentary system was changing everything from black and white to somewhere in-between. Aside from indignation about the prime minister's concessions to the Labour members, the bill was criticized on other grounds. The argument that a pension would discourage thrift was still made, to which a member who supported the bill replied: "…[T]hat idea was prevalent at the time women wore crinolines, and I think it went out about the same time as crinolines did." One member was concerned that pension legislation would advertise to the world that Canada afforded so narrow a margin between income and living costs that the state had to step in and maintain its elderly population. And there were many who felt, because the proposed old age pension system was based on federal-provincial cost-sharing, that the approval of all provinces should be sought before federal legislation was passed.

Media reaction was mixed. The *Montreal Gazette* noted that the bill was not making much progress and added: "There seems to be no recognized demand for it." The *Sydney Post* declared: "There is not an important newspaper in the country, Liberal or Conservative, which has shown any enthusiasm for this hastily prepared and imperfectly drafted measure." On the other hand, the *Toronto Globe* received several 'letters to the editor' from Ontario residents who were watching the progress of the bill with high expectations. One letter-writer, looking ahead to Ontario's role in taking up the offer of shared funding of old age pensions, described the activities of his group which was already circulating petitions. He went on to report:

> We also intend in the near future to have an automobile parade through the city which, besides giving the old people an enjoyable outing, will focus public attention on our efforts to compel the Provincial Government to do its obvious duty by joining the central Government...

Despite its rough treatment in the House and mixed reaction in the press, there was not a single vote against the pension bill when it was passed. This was evidently not one of those occasions when the government's minority position made the slightest difference. After almost 20 years, the House had finally passed old age pension legislation. Few of the elderly who had their hopes raised in 1907 were still around to witness the approval of Canada's first federal social program. Although it was a start, the program still reflected the reluctance of Canadian society to give hand-outs if work was even a remote possibility. Pensions would be paid only to those over 70 years of age (at a time when life expectancies were lower than today) and to those who passed a means test. From coast to coast newspapers dutifully reported the result, but there was little fanfare about this historic milestone, and it was just as well. Only 11 days later the Senate rejected the bill, bringing down upon itself the wrath of both major parties and stunned silence from Progressive and Labour members whose learning curve with regard to the ways of government was now almost complete.

The Senate rejection was based on several arguments, but the lack of prior provincial approval for a cost-shared program was the major criticism. There were also concerns about the fate of Canada if children were no longer to be responsible for their elderly parents. With their own incomes securely in place for life, the senators failed to predict how the general public would react to their rejection of pensions for the working class. The *Toronto Globe* described public sentiment:

> Criticism of the Senate has been revived in a vigorous manner in various parts of Canada...The long record of opposition to reform measures is recalled and the question is once more asked: When and how can the Senate be brought more into conformity with modern thought and methods of government?

In the House a B.C. member described the attitude of the average Canadian toward the Senate as "one of mild derision, rising in some cases to hostile dimensions," and warned that senators had been short-sighted. Imagining himself a member of that body, he went on to observe that:

> ....[I]f I were animated only by a selfish desire to remain in the promised land as long as I could until death might us part, my one last and only advice to my fellow members would be "Pass this measure, and pass it quickly, for if you don't the people will turn on us and rend us and we shall be torn apart from the emoluments we receive."

It was the following year before the bill was re-introduced in the House and forwarded again to the Senate. By that time an uncomfortable feeling permeated the upper chamber, a strong suspicion that the previous rejection of the bill may have added fuel to the ever-present threat of Senate reform. This time it was dutifully passed, and the Old Age Pensions Act of 1927 became law.

•••

Though Mackenzie King was criticized both in the House and Senate for introducing legislation that was merely a concession to the small Labour Party, a few, albeit *very* few, members argued that this was an acceptable, even desirable, way of conducting the business of government. One member reminded his colleagues:

On both sides of the House there are many members who owe a large measure of their support to labour…I do not know that it would be a very great crime if the government yielded to wishes presented by a considerable section of the House in reference to legislation.

The presence rather than the size of third parties in the House was beginning to affect the actions of the old parties as it would continue to affect future Canadian parliaments. Although Labour members had pushed the prime minister to present the bill, the unanimous response to the third reading indicated their votes were not even needed. Their greatest contribution had been prying the bill out of the back rooms into the light of day where both old parties were forced to debate it in full view of the public. A whole range of social issues awaited this kind of airing but had failed to receive it in the traditional two-party system. The passing of old age pension legislation showed the Labour members how it could be done — the presence of a third party was the key.

It had become clear that neither of the existing Progressive or Labour parties would be the third party to take on this role in the long term. Five years earlier they had entered Parliament with separate interests, but the situation changed as many of the Progressives drifted back into the Liberal fold. By 1924 the hard-core Progressives who refused to be lured back had developed a cooperative working relationship with the Labour members. On issues of injustice toward less powerful groups in Canadian society, they found themselves on the same side. This often meant farmer representatives voted on behalf of workingmen, a possibility they would have denied when they were first elected. As time went on they began to meet in unofficial joint caucuses. The combined strength of the small group was not lost on the two older parties which showed their discomfort either by name-calling ("radicals and Bolshevists") or condescension ("I am largely of the opinion that one good crop in the West — let us pray heaven that it comes this year — will remove very much of the irritation that exists among our Western friends.").

Though they nettled the older parties, the Progressive and Labour members were a political alliance, not yet a formal political party with a mandate that extended beyond sectional or regional interests. Within five years, however, the informal caucus meetings became planning sessions for a national party. The continued growth of labour unions and farmers' associations throughout the country and the sudden impact of the Depression gave an impetus to party organization. At a 1932 conference in Calgary the greatly expanded group developed a provisional framework for the new party (to be called the Co-operative Commonwealth Federation), with J.S. Woodsworth as its leader. A year later it held the first annual party convention. This challenge to the old two-party system, accompanied by changing public attitudes arising out of the realities of the Depression, would force new issues onto the parliamentary agenda. Over the next 10 years both major parties, in turn, would introduce social welfare reforms which would have been totally unacceptable to the House and public alike in the previous decade.

CHAPTER 4

The Decade of Misery

After the relative prosperity of the mid-1920s, the Depression appeared with suddenness and severity. By the spring of 1930 most Canadians living in cities could see with their own eyes the evidence of large-scale unemployment. In their own way rural Canadians were also suffering. There had been a poor wheat crop in the fall and ineffective marketing of what crops there were. The unemployed in the cities were even led to believe that the two were connected — the poor crop and unemployment — and that jobs would soon be available when wheat started to roll again.

But there had been crop failures before. Never had they created conditions across the country like those of the spring of 1930 when unemployment normally experienced in winter months stretched on into the months of mild weather. In Toronto thousands of unemployed men, many described as being in a state of destitution, crowded into employment offices only to be turned away when no jobs became available. In March the city's House of Industry provided more meals to men out of work than ever before in its history. Further north in Ontario, the Collingwood newspaper reported:

....[Y]oung men, clean limbed and able workers, arrive each day, penniless and hungry at the Orillia jail with a plea for a night out of the cold and a breakfast in the morning.

In Ottawa the Union Mission declared that in no previous spring in memory had its hostel for indigent men been so crowded. And in Fort William unemployed workers organized parades through the streets.

The situation in the West was so serious that western mayors and provincial representatives called a conference in Winnipeg to deal with the problem of massive numbers of men out of work. In Edmonton the municipality and the province of Alberta were feeding 4,000 single men and 400 married men with their families. Also in Alberta, in the Drumheller mining area, 80 percent of miners were reported to be out of work. Unemployed men in Winnipeg waited in a breadline, four deep and two blocks long, as many as 3,000 being fed in a given day. And as a result of the short crop of 1929, large numbers of people in Saskatchewan were out of work.

In the Maritimes the miners of Cape Breton had been working on average one-and-a-half days a week during the winter due to lack of markets. In the spring one of New Brunswick's largest newsprint mills reduced its operations to two or three days a week, throwing at least 1,500 people out of work.

In April the *Montreal Gazette* reported that 1,132 men were lined up at a downtown soup kitchen on one day. Serious unemployment in the areas north and northeast of the city prompted the passing of a Montreal by-law to prevent any outsider from getting work in the city. It was also reported that many Caughnawaga Indians formerly employed by the Dominion Bridge Company and other construction companies in Montreal were unemployed, causing conditions that were a threat to health on the Caughnawaga reserve. In the northern townships of Quebec the situation was no better. There was no activity in cutting pulpwood or hardwood, and all lumber yards were said to be filled with the previous year's cut.

These were the early months of the Depression. The public had still not grasped its depth, nor even guessed what would be its duration. In fact, public attitudes toward unemployment and the unemployed had not changed significantly from the attitudes held at the turn of the century. Able-bodied men were expected to find work, and the belief still prevailed that men without jobs were simply malingering. In that case the worst possible solution was to give a hand-out. "Unemployment relief is simply an encouragement to more unemployment" was the argument made by public officials at a federal-provincial conference in the late 1920s. The situation still did not warrant a change in this guiding philosophy.

Although public attitudes were reminiscent of 1900, there had been occasions over the previous 30 years when restrictions on granting outdoor relief had been relaxed. Soup kitchens had appeared in Toronto in 1908 during a period of recession and high unemployment when 1,500 workingmen and their families ("shackers" living on the outskirts of the city, according to the *Toronto Globe*) received food, clothing, and household supplies without being required to enter the county workhouse. In the same city in the severe unemployment of 1914, the *Globe* reported that there were 15,000 men walking the streets. On that occasion private charities distributed provisions to needy families and the *Globe* called for action from city officials in providing jobs through public works.

By the time the postwar depression of 1919 to 1923 arrived, the pattern of emergency relief had been established — private-charity responsibility for food, clothing, and often shelter (in privately operated missions) and municipal responsibility for providing what public works the municipality could afford. But the postwar depression affecting thousands of returning soldiers was more than this division of labour could handle. The resources of private charities were soon depleted and the burden for both relief and public works fell on municipal authorities. The municipalities, strained to the limit within a few short months, turned to the provinces for assistance. They, in turn, looked to the federal government.

By this chain of events the federal government was drawn into providing financial assistance for the unemployed (one-third of the cost of relief) long before the introduction of old age pensions in 1927 and the onset of the Depression in 1930. Given public attitudes about outdoor relief, there seemed to be three reasons, one stated and two unstated, for this unprecedented action. Since many of the unemployed were returning soldiers, federal assistance for relief had been justified as part of an overall policy of helping to re-establish war veterans. This was the stated reason. But there was also some uneasiness about the anger and distrust that had given rise to the Winnipeg General Strike. Hostility may well have gone underground following the government's repressive measures. If so, there was nothing to say it would remain there permanently, and there was no eagerness to see it surface again. Concessions to frustrated and angry unemployed workers could be timely and effective.

A third reason for federal government assistance in 1921 was the pressure over five years for a system of state insurance against unemployment. The Social Service Congresses of 1914 and 1916 and the government's own Royal Commission on Industrial Relations in 1919 had pushed for such a system. Grants-in-aid for relief costs represented a simpler, less expensive way of responding to the problem and might diffuse temporarily the agitation for a state unemployment insurance plan. For all these reasons the federal government agreed to help municipalities with relief costs, calling its assistance "emergency" relief to emphasize its temporary nature. It continued to provide help from 1921 to 1927.

This was the history of reluctant federal involvement in assistance to the unemployed when the stock market crashed near the end of 1929. Despite reports of hardship from coast to coast throughout the following winter and spring, the federal government went through a period of denial. The 1930 throne speech was filled with glowing references to Canada's economic prosperity. Challenged about the widespread suffering and privation, Prime Minister Mackenzie King claimed that the stock market collapse had merely affected the fortunes of individuals. "But it did not at all affect the soundness of business in this country;" he said, "it in no way is a factor which has contributed to any permanent set-back." As a matter of fact, he added, it could prove to be a very good thing.

Non-government members of the House of Commons pressed for a contribution to the burden of relief being carried by the municipalities and provinces. As if to underline that unemployment was not a serious problem, the government insisted that the provinces and municipalities were not asking for help. There were also demands, especially from the small group of Labour members, for the introduction of unemployment insurance, the now familiar state insurance proposal which had reappeared again in the recommendations of a 1929 select committee. The response was that an unemployment insurance scheme was constitutionally a provincial responsibility. (This had also been the position taken by the select committee.) And, the government's spokesman added, unemployment insurance would only be adopted in Canada after public opinion had been educated to the necessity for it.

Editorials in Canadian newspapers confirmed this view of lukewarm public opinion about unemployment insurance. The *Montreal Gazette* asked:

> Whither are we drifting in this matter of socialistic paternalism?...While human nature remains as it is, and as it has been through the centuries, it is sheer madness to tell idle and shiftless men and women that the state will step in and save them from the penalties of their violation of fixed social laws.

The *Halifax Chronicle* was unenthusiastic for other reasons. Referring to the unemployment question being debated in the House, the *Chronicle* commented:

> What should be done about it? Unemployment insurance? But is that a remedy? As a treatment of symptoms it deserves consideration — as a remedy it has not even the virtue of a rabbit's foot.

Although unemployment insurance had few supporters, there were expectations of federal contributions to relief. The *Edmonton Journal* took the government to task for its claim that provinces were not asking for financial help with relief costs and pointed to the volume of protest against government inaction that had been heard in Alberta. The economic situation had placed an unfair burden for relief on provinces and municipalities. "The Dominion," the *Journal* contended, "is evading its share of responsibility."

The *Manitoba Free Press* reported that the Manitoba premier had indeed pressed for federal aid in meeting the cost of relief and assured its readers that "assistance for the Western municipalities and provinces in bearing their load at the present time is to be expected from the Dominion Government."

With a choice of three options — the short-term option of assisting with emergency relief costs, the longer-term option of introducing a federal system of unemployment insurance, and sitting tight — the Liberal government chose to sit tight. There were many more months of nationwide distress before an election was called and a Conservative government took office. The new prime minister, R.B. Bennett, a self-willed man, a parliamentarian of tradition but a one-man show within his own cabinet, faced the country with confidence but not much warmth. He may have considered the same three options. By the time he took office in the summer of 1930, however, the third option was out of the question. At a special session in the fall, the House passed Bennett's legislation to provide $20 million to the provinces and municipalities to help with relief work projects and direct relief costs. A bill raising tariff levels aimed at stimulating the economy was also passed.

Public reaction was generally favourable toward the proposed $20 million expenditure. With the government's emphasis on public works construction projects (and its strategy of downplaying the contribution to direct relief), there was a certain amount of vagueness about how the funds would be spent. This allowed everyone to see some good in it. The general public still wanted the unemployed to be put to work rather than given hand-outs, and funding of public works would create jobs. The unemployed also preferred jobs, not more soup kitchens and breadlines. The provinces and municipalities wanted help with uncontrollable expenditures on direct relief. They would now receive a third of the costs from the federal government. Industrial interests wanted assurance that any measures to help unemployed workers would be short term for all the reasons of work incentive well-known since the beginning of the century. They were satisfied the direct relief section of the legislation was a temporary expedient to meet a national emergency.

The *Montreal Gazette*, for example, was eloquent in its praise of the new tariff legislation which it called a permanent remedy for unemployment. It even accepted the funding of public works and direct relief, both of which were considered "necessarily temporary in character" and "designed to give immediate relief." But the omission of unemployment insurance from the government's new proposals was good news to the *Gazette* which carried an ominous warning from a visiting British industrialist that unemployment insurance would slow down industry and promote laziness.

According to the *Québec Événement*, it was not just workers who would take advantage of the public with unemployment insurance. Big industrial corporations could throw hundreds of thousands of their employees on the street and the government would tax the rest of the country to pay for it. Moreover:

> ....[I]f by the combined influence of selfish employers and unthinking workers the state is forced to assume their social obligations, the farmers and the country people who form the majority of our population would be justified in organizing to demand government benefits.

In fact, there was never a risk of unemployment insurance appearing among the proposals of the new government. Before the special session of the House opened in the fall, the minister of labour, Gideon Robertson, had convened the Economic Service Council of Canada, an advisory group of representatives from provincial governments, business, agriculture, and labour. With an opening statement that the government did not propose to "extend paternalism" to the unemployed, the minister asked for recommendations to deal with the economic crisis. The only issue causing a sharp division among the council members was unemployment insurance which, supported by labour and opposed by business leaders, was finally deleted from the list of proposals.

As the Depression deepened federal government measures to deal with it became ineffective. By 1931 tariffs had failed to stimulate industrial growth, public works had failed to make a substantial dent in unemployment, and federal funds to help municipalities with relief were almost exhausted. An estimated 250,000 Canadians were out of work. Moreover, the frustration of unemployed workers was growing by the day and there were incidents of disorder reported by many government employment centres.

The provinces and municipalities waited anxiously for word of renewed federal funding. Though a year's experience had shown that many public works projects were a costly way of putting food in people's mouths, it was still the method preferred by the general public. But the public was now beginning to see these projects in a different light, not so much as a better alternative than a hand-out, but as a solution to the hardship they saw increasing by the day. According to the *Vancouver Province*, despite doubts about value-for-dollar, money for public works was money well spent:

> It is desirable at all times to get value for public money. But it is more desirable that our people should not be allowed to starve. It is desirable, likewise, in public financing to balance the budget. But it is more desirable, in an emergency like the present, to maintain our people on a self-respecting basis.

By summer new relief legislation was introduced in Parliament, this time including measures for farmers as well as wage-earners. There was no question of public works projects for stricken farmers. Relief for rural families was to be direct in the form of food and fuel, and not a single public comment appeared in opposition to what was clearly a hand-out. Given the reality of dust storms and scanty crops, the *Toronto Telegram* stated:

> ....[T]here is no use moralizing. It is a case of whether Canadians will sit by and see their fellow citizens in actual want.

In the same vein the *Ottawa Journal* observed:

> From coast to coast newspapers of all shades of politics rally behind the government's decision to help the West. There is, despite everything, a spirit of unity in Canada.

Under the new legislation make-work projects would continue for the thousands of urban unemployed. Labour members continued to push for unemployment insurance, but it was late in the day for insurance. The pressing need was to put out the fire. For workers who would not be absorbed by public works, direct relief would be available, but there was less talk now about its effect on the incentive to work and more talk about responding to the hunger of a large portion of the Canadian population.

Responding to hunger was the primary goal. But there were also appeals for more considerate treatment of the unemployed, especially those travelling across the country in search of work, and a growing recognition that they were not to blame for their plight. The *Regina Leader* could see nothing to be proud of in current practices. "In cities and towns all over the Dominion," the *Leader* reported, "men are picked up by the police, kept overnight, and given so many hours to get out of town." Perhaps the most eloquent plea was made by the *Vancouver Province* which argued that the "drifter" had received only a minimum of consideration in the crisis. Reminding Canadians that the drifter was very much a part of Canada's history — the early coureurs-de-bois, later the explorers of the Northwest, the nineteenth-century railway builders, the first pioneers of the plains, all drifters in one way or another — the *Province* went on:

> As for the drifters of our own day, who are they?...Just the sort of men who have built Canada from the ground up, and the sort we shall need in the future if we are to make further progress. It ill becomes the Canada of 1931, the creation of whole generations of drifters, to be contemptuous of the drifter of today because he lacks the price of a meal or a place to lay his head.

While new relief funding for unemployed workers was good news in the House and across the country, there was mixed reaction to another proposal. In announcing a continuation of relief the government asked for unlimited spending power, a measure not even granted for defence expenditures during the war. In addition, it asked for broader powers for the maintenance of peace and order, conceivably to suppress threats of unrest that might arise. In the House of Commons other parties strongly opposed these extraordinary powers, but the measure was passed. The press, on the other hand, was not unanimously against granting unlimited spending. The *Victoria Times* came out against it:

> Nobody has the faintest idea of what the government

proposes to do. It has said to Parliament, in effect, give us power to take all the money we want and leave the rest to us.

And the *Vancouver Province* took the other side. But the *Province*, like many other newspapers, was against the powers granted for the maintenance of peace and order:

> The Prime Minister has made a good case for the "blank cheque" legislation he is asking. There is an emergency which demands emergency measures. His case for extraordinary police powers is not by any means so good. There is no emergency in the country such as the request for such powers would suggest.

It was still only the beginning. The federal government would introduce new relief legislation each year for the next four years. At no time was there a master plan — new legislation was enacted as time limits on the old ran out and as the economy failed to make the upturn the government hoped for with each passing year. By 1932 there were an estimated 400,000 unemployed across the country. In Saskatchewan, following three successive years of crop failures, over 300,000 farm people, nearly one-third of the province's population, were assisted with medical services, food, and fuel, much of the assistance funded fully by the federal government.

By 1933 over 750,000 people were without jobs. The government extended the relief legislation for another year. The leader of the opposition in the House made a pledge that if his party were returned to power he would institute a system of unemployment insurance, the same measure he refused to institute in the late 1920s for constitutional reasons.

By 1934 one-and-a-third million men, women, and children, or 13.5 percent of the total population of Canada, were living on relief. It is possible the reality of this figure was not known to some Canadians, but there were few unaware that thousands of the country's young men, riding on top of railway boxcars, were moving back and forth across the country looking for work. These young men were not merely statistics of able-bodied prime-working-age unemployed; they were sons of working-class and middle-class Canadians, and nearly everyone knew someone in this unprecedented situation. With such general firsthand experience, public attitudes began to harden against the failure of business and government to turn things around.

The Conservatives finally came up with a long-term plan in 1935. But the proposals were so uncharacteristic of the party's traditional opposition to paternalism that many saw the plan as a government attempt to distance itself from business, or at least its close alliance with business in the public's mind. It had all the earmarks of a strategy of desperation in an election year that followed five long years of deteriorating economic conditions.

Even the way the prime minister chose to announce the new plan was uncharacteristic. Bennett, the man of tradition, was the first Canadian politician to use a series of radio broadcasts to announce a government program. (But he was not the first in North America to realize the political potential of radio, an invention then in use commercially for only 15 years. U.S. President Franklin Delano Roosevelt had already held radio "fireside chats" with his fellow Americans and Fiorella La Guardia, mayor of New York City, could be tuned in on Sunday mornings for his weekly reading of the comic pages.) When he spoke to the country, Bennett made a promise to his stunned listeners to reform the capitalist economic system and introduce government regulation of business. It was a system, he said, that had brought unparalleled disaster. In addition to these sweeping proposals, he promised specific reforms — a minimum wage and a maximum work week, unemployment insurance, a contributory pension system, and health insurance — all of which might have been "blunders" if instituted earlier in the Depression for reasons that were beyond his control:

> This Government was not long in office before demands for reform were made upon it. Such demands were natural. But in your interest, they could not then be heeded. The ship was pounding in mountainous seas. That was not the time to try to recondition it.

But now (although many would have argued the seas were still mountainous) he was determined to set things right. After five years of holding to a policy of emergency relief, the prime minister made an incredible admission. "The dole is a rotten thing," he said. "It is alike an insult to the worker and to those who profess to have control of our industrial system." Not surprisingly, his newfound reform agenda came as a shock to Canadians who were tuned in from coast to coast. The proposed reforms, the prime minister's publicity officer commented in a mild understatement, were "a notable departure from traditional Conservative Party policy."

Press reaction ranged from cynicism to outrage, depending on the political leaning of the newspaper. The *Halifax Chronicle* simply refused to believe the prime minister's change of heart. "As to reform, we believe in reform," the *Chronicle* said, "but we do not believe in Mr. Bennett as a reformer." The *Toronto Globe* was less inclined to doubt the sincerity of the proposals and had no problem with their substance. They showed the prime minister had become radical, "but not reckless." The *Globe* argued:

> Most of the points disclosed — if not all of them — are capable of treatment by legislation which would not be revolutionary.

The *Winnipeg Free Press* refused to give Bennett credit for becoming radical, finding something suspicious in his sudden discovery that the capitalist system was so defective and injurious that something would have to be done about it. "What new or radical revolution in capitalism is needed to install or improve social legislation of this type?" asked the *Free Press*.

The editor of the conservative *Montreal Gazette* was apoplectic:

> ....[B]e it noted that the Prime Minister puts forward his new policy not as representing the considered judgment of his party, which would be impossible, but as something of his own; it might, indeed, be called the policy of the first person singular.

The *Gazette* criticized the policy as socialistic and denounced unemployment insurance as ineffective, just as it had claimed in the early years of the Depression.

Following his radio announcements in January, Bennett introduced the Employment and Social Insurance Act in the House of Commons in March, but time was running out on the governing party which was required to go to the polls after five years in office. The election in the fall was notable for several reasons. First, despite the prime minister's last-ditch conversion to reform policies, his party failed to return to power. It was replaced by a Liberal government. And second, the new CCF party gained seats in the first election since its creation in 1933, though not as many seats as its members had hoped. Affecting the election outcome for both the Conservatives and the CCF was a new Alberta-based Social Credit Party, which won the votes of the disenchanted in Alberta that might otherwise have gone to the other two parties.

For the unemployed who might have been looking to the central government for solutions, the remaining five years of the decade (and of the Depression) were a disappointment. Direct relief continued, and fewer public works projects, but the unemployment insurance bill introduced by the former government had many political and legal obstacles to overcome before it would ever see the light of day. Sent to both the Supreme Court of Canada and the Privy Council to test its legality, the bill was in abeyance for almost two years before the ruling was made that it was in conflict with the provisions of the British North America Act.

Since the constitutional problem specifically related to the respective jurisdictions of federal and provincial governments, a royal commission was appointed to examine the whole division of responsibilities (and taxing powers) between the two levels, especially the ability of the provinces to finance the matters under their authority. While the commission carried out its mandate, the federal government sought approval of the provinces individually to amend the constitution to allow it to introduce an unemployment insurance program. The large majority of the provinces were prepared to amend without delay. Still, both of these federal initiatives, the commission's work and the negotiations with all nine provinces, took another three years. By 1940, when the way was clear to go ahead with a constitutional amendment and a new Unemployment Insurance Act, the country was at war. Canadians watched the unemployed join the armed forces and watched the unemployment problem vanish. But memories were long. There was strong support for any program that would prevent the hardship and deprivation of the past 10 years. Although some sectors of business were still against the proposal, and although Prime Minister MacKenzie King admitted later to opposition from his own cabinet, the bill went through the House with relative ease. The Senate, after considerable debate, also gave its approval.

"The Senate would have been ill-advised to hold up the unemployment insurance bill," commented the *Edmonton Journal*, and this was typical of the acceptance of the new legislation by the press across the country. The war had pushed unemployment off the front pages. Most newspapers let the final assent to the Unemployment Insurance Act of 1940 pass without comment.

It was 20 years since unemployment insurance had been first proposed in the House of Commons, 20 years of delay for constitutional reasons. Or was the constitution really to blame? There is strong evidence that the legislation would never have received broad public support earlier. In 1927 officials at a federal-provincial conference claimed unemployment insurance led to even more unemployment. Three years later, in the first year of the Depression, the public still believed help for the unemployed should be restricted to emergencies. And the government, sensitive to public opinion, announced its measures would not "extend paternalism" to those out of work. It was only as the disastrous conditions of the Depression unfolded, as Canadians began to see that the system had broken down and the unemployed were not to blame, that attitudes began to change. But when the country threw out one party in 1935 and voted in another, the new prime minister had every reason to believe that unemployment insurance, the much-publicized legislation he inherited from the defeated government, was still not popular in some areas, especially the business community. Why offend business when, in fact, it might catch up with the rest of public opinion in time? King had enacted old age pension legislation in 1927 without provincial approval, but now he made jurisdictional issues a *cause célèbre* and gained five more years. In the end he never completely gained the support of business, but with the general public strongly on his side and the war about to satisfy industrial interests by turning the economy around, 1940 was a year when he could safely move ahead without their support.

CHAPTER 5

Postwar Plans:
Victim of Power Struggles

The Depression left in its wake an almost permanent pessimism in many Canadians. Business prospered in wartime as it often does, unemployment declined, and federal taxation powers brought in unprecedented revenues. Still the breadlines and the soup kitchens were not easily forgotten and the shift to prosperity was seen by many as transitory. It would all end when the war was over. Wasn't that exactly what had happened following World War I?

The government seemed determined not to repeat the mistakes of World War I, but its plans for postwar reconstruction received mixed reviews. At the federal level a planning committee of academic, business, and labour people was set up. Strongly influenced by the broad social security proposals being considered in Great Britain (the Beveridge Plan), the committee developed a similar blueprint for Canada. The main features of the plan, named after its author Leonard Marsh and introduced in the spring of 1943, included monthly payments to every Canadian family for each child under 16 — a baby bonus — and a system of national health insurance.

But in Central Canada these plans were seen as pie in the sky. The general feeling was that they would never even get off the ground in the depressed economic conditions that were certain to return at the end of the war. The Toronto *Globe and Mail* outlined the proposals and cautioned readers that the state could only spend what people earned:

The people collectively will have to work and produce far more than they did before the war to finance extensive Government-directed assistance for themselves.

The *Ottawa Citizen* was completely negative, calling the social security plan "rationed poverty":

....[S]lice it how you will, it is still no more than a scheme for spreading the burden of poverty wider...it bears little relationship to Canada as a land of plenty.

Under the somewhat cynical heading "Won't It Be Wonderful?" the *Montreal Gazette* warned, "...[T]here is one comment which applies not only to Dr. Marsh's reasoning but to any social insurance scheme: It does NOT represent Utopia." In the same vein the *Ottawa Journal* was anxious not to inflate hopes:

Unless by international agreement we can find some way to sell our products abroad following the war, Canada will not be in a position to pay for social security. That is as clear as that two and two makes four.

Out west the editorials were a little less gloomy. After noting that the plan was being received with caution by some Canadians, the *Calgary Herald* observed: "The road toward yesterday's headlines may be long and bumpy, but most people believe it can be negotiated." The *Winnipeg Free Press* reported that both the Manitoba Medical Association and Alberta Medical Association found the health insurance proposal sound. The *Free Press* contended that, in general, the country was ready for a much improved and more scientific system of social security. The *Vancouver Province* called the Marsh plan imaginative, yet realistic; the *Edmonton Journal* commented that the fundamental principle of guaranteeing to each citizen a minimum subsistence was now accepted by most Canadians. The *Victoria Times* had praise for the whole planning process:

Canada knows to her cost what price she paid for failure to anticipate the problems associated with demobilization a quarter of a century ago...it is to be hoped Parliament and people will regard [the proposals] as beacons pointing the way to a new order...

Hardest hit by the Depression, Western Canada still wanted desperately to see a silver lining that Eastern Canada could not see. But for all Canadians postwar plans would have to take second place to their preoccupation with getting sons and husbands home safely from the battlefields in Europe, Asia, and North Africa. By late spring 1943 the issue of the direction Canada would take with social security had dropped off the public agenda.

In the fall rumours about imminent government action on the baby bonus were rampant enough for the press to take up the controversy again. On the heels of a recommendation from the National War Labour Board for substantial wage increases across the country — in other words, removal of the wartime wage freeze — the government was forced to give serious consideration to alternatives that would not so readily lead to inflation. Or so the rumours went.

It was difficult to determine the reaction of the general public amid the hue and cry that followed in the press. Despite all the publicity given to the government's postwar plans in the spring, the *Financial Post* called the proposal for family allowances (the more formal name for the baby bonus) "revolutionary." The *Montreal Gazette* argued the time was all wrong for such a measure. The *Globe and Mail* also asked "Why now?" There was still uneasiness about the country's ability to finance such a scheme in the postwar period. The *Globe* favoured a subsidy "directly into the pay envelope" that could be discontinued by industry when warranted. The *Vancouver Province* claimed: "A system of family allowances smacks of relief rolls and is repugnant to Canadian ideals." The *Edmonton Journal* urged everyone to relax. The government would surely encourage the widest discussion in Parliament and throughout the country before making "such a radical departure."

The truth was family allowances were indeed being discussed in cabinet and, as Prime Minister Mackenzie King reported later, several key cabinet members were against such a program. But the man who had so skilfully taken the public's temperature on unemployment insurance during the 1930s was certain that a family allowance program would be popular with the vast majority of Canadians in the mid-1940s. He was impatient with Liberal colleagues who failed to see a threat in the recent successes of the CCF party. Besides forming the government in Saskatchewan in June 1944, it had become the official opposition in Ontario during the summer and in recent federal by-elections had won two former Liberal seats. When discussion of family allowances moved to the caucus, King found as much division on the subject as in cabinet earlier. He reported the heated discussion in his diary, including his final words. Unless they were willing to allow the CCF to sweep the country and take measures that would be extreme, he warned caucus members, they must keep liberal principles continually to the fore. Opinion polls during the fall showed that King had retained his skill in reading the public. Though no legislation had yet been introduced, 49 percent of Canadians were in favour of family allowances compared to 42 percent opposed.

King almost personally pushed through the family allowance proposal over the next seven or eight months. Ready to take on the 42 percent opposed to the proposal, he geared himself for charges of paternalism and even for attitudes dredged up from the past that cash in the hands of some individuals would be ill spent. There was indeed criticism on these grounds. The *Montreal Gazette* reminded its readers of the hungry '30s:

> Money was being handed out in every direction...Individual initiative was being stifled by this pathetic paternalism. It was a national experiment that had tragic consequences for all because billions of dollars were distributed and at the end there was nothing to show for the process. And once more that policy is to be given a trial.

And some Canadians still believed that low-income families were unable to manage their money. In Ontario a *Midland Free Press Herald* editorial commented:

> One could wish that it was possible for such grants to really go to the children in better food, clothing and educational opportunities. Instead, we are afraid a great deal of it will

find its way to the beverage rooms which are one reason why many fathers, otherwise good, remain in the low-wage group.

And these fears were not confined to small-town Ontario. The Toronto *Globe and Mail* also doubted the distributed money would serve its intended purpose:

> What guarantee can there be that it will provide the additional nutritional foods the family needs, that it will be used for necessary medical and child care, or to keep the children at school or to provide decent, adequate housing?

In the same vein the *Ottawa Citizen* claimed the prime minister's scheme contained "no guarantee that a single nickel will go to improve the lot of the children."

Although King was prepared to defend the "humble poor" (as he called them in the House) against such attitudes, he met his greatest opposition from another front entirely. In Ontario, in particular, attempts to scuttle the family allowance proposal took the form of well-placed arguments that the greatest benefit would be to Quebec, a province of historically large families, while Ontario would shoulder the burden of costs. This was, in fact, the nature of the discussion in the Liberal caucus itself which prompted King to lecture caucus members about the CCF threat. The suggestion that other Canadians would be paying for the large families of Quebec spread to Manitoba where the *Brandon Sun* took it up:

> The rest of Canada could with some justice assert that the baby bonus was taken from them for the main benefit of the province of Quebec.

The federal opposition added fuel to the fire when its leader, John Bracken, labelled the family allowance proposal "a political bribe" to ensure Liberal votes in Quebec. Commissioned by the opposition party to review the Marsh proposals, Charlotte Whitton, former director of the Canadian Welfare Council, pointed out in an additional pamphlet that the average number of children in families of British descent was 2.86 compared to 4.28 in families of French descent. "It is neither dishonourable nor mischievous frankly to face these facts for they are of grave import," she said. Others argued that higher birth rates in Quebec (encouraged by family allowances) would ultimately lead to the end of the predominance of Anglo-Saxon stock in Canada.

While these sentiments were being circulated in an effort to stir up opposition, the *Halifax Chronicle* calmly pointed out that there were 1.1 million children eligible for the baby bonus in Quebec and 1.05 million eligible in Ontario. The *Regina Leader-Post* reported that Quebec led Ontario in the matter of families with more than four children by a margin of less than 15 percent. The *Chronicle* also put in its own dig at those complaining about one-sided benefits for Quebec:

> ...[T]he obvious answer to that criticism is that it would be a good thing for this country if the English-speaking part of our citizenry went back to the good old-fashioned theory of bringing up large families.

Other critics of the proposition that family allowances would end the predominance of Anglo-Saxon stock pointed out that, regardless of family allowances, the Anglo-Saxon population in Canada was not reproducing itself at a sufficient rate to ensure its continuity. Moreover, the effects of urbanization and industrialization operating in French Canada over two or three decades had been to lower birth rates in Quebec at a faster rate than the decline outside Quebec.[4] No measure of social security, not even the baby bonus, would be able to offset the influence of such powerful factors.

The family allowance proposal weathered the storm generated by the opposition. It was not an example of Canadians at their best. With cabinet and caucus finally onside, the prime minister introduced the bill in the summer of 1944 and, within a few short weeks, opposition members were aware of the bill's popularity among their own constituents. Rumours spread quickly that, despite their leader's strong statements about political bribery, many in the opposition were reluctant to vote against it and agreed within the party not to take part in the second-reading debate. It was a remarkable outcome for one of Canada's earliest social programs. The prime minister wrote later:

> ...[W]e compelled a vote on the second reading. It was one I shall never forget; one that will not be forgotten in the records of Canada's Parliament. Every member in the House, of all parties, supported the measure — 139 to nil was the vote recorded.

The first family allowances were distributed to Canadian mothers the following year. In the years that followed the program was proudly held up as Canada's first "universal" social program, that is, an allowance distributed to all families regardless of income. But family allowances were never intended to help middle- and upper-income Canadians. Benefits were aimed at the range of workers whose wages were inequitably low due to the wartime freeze. So low were their wages, in fact, that they paid no income tax and could not be helped by the exemption in respect of children given to taxpayers. In exchange for receiving family allowances, middle- and upper-income Canadians would forfeit the former tax exemptions. Most Canadians were aware of this trade-off. Certainly the prime minister knew the public was not ready for universality. He argued that "to tell the country that everyone was to get a family allowance was sheer folly; it would occasion resentment everywhere." In his speeches in the House, family allowances and "the poor" were clearly linked.

The allowances, then, were actually another step in Canada's recognition of its responsibility for the poor. Despite the partisan bickering that surrounded any piece of new legislation, most Canadians were ready to assume the responsibility. As the *Victoria Times* noted, "the steady growth in public sentiment in favour of a greater measure of social security dates from the beginning of the century." One could argue with the word "steady," but it was true three major federal programs and three provincial programs were now in place where none existed at the turn of the century.

•••

It is hardly world-shattering news that on occasion politicians let their own power struggles deflect them from the course of responding to public opinion. It was clear in the 1940s that the public wanted greater government involvement in social security. Unemployment insurance legislation ran into very little resistance once the constitution was amended; family allowances even won opposition votes in the end. A Gallup poll of 1944 indicated that 80 percent of Canadians were in favour of a national health plan. Yet those in positions of power managed to fumble the health insurance proposals that had also been a major part of the 1943 Marsh report.

The constitution permitted a program of family allowances at the federal level without jurisdictional challenges; the allowances were deemed to be gifts with no federal intention of entering a provincial field. But the introduction of a national health program was another matter. The responsibility for health issues clearly belonged to the provinces while the federal role was confined to grants-in-aid. National unemployment insurance had required agreement from the provinces to a constitutional amendment, a process that had taken five years, but there was little likelihood of provincial agreement in the case of health. This division of responsibility, however, did not preclude leadership by the federal government in initiating a national grants proposal that would encourage provinces to set up their own health insurance programs. And this is what the federal government set out to do in 1945.

The Dominion-Provincial Conference on Reconstruction was called to look at a whole range of postwar issues, one of which was health insurance. The re-establishment of war veterans, housing, industry, agriculture, and wage controls were all on the agenda, but the most important item was agreement between the federal and provincial governments on future financial arrangements. In 1941 the provinces had transferred to the federal government their rights to collect personal and corporation income taxes for the duration of the war (and up to one year after). This was now up for discussion. With these and other revenue sources, the federal government had grown in strength *vis-à-vis* the provinces. The year 1945 heralded the beginning of the long struggle to reverse this power balance.

At the dominion-provincial conference the federal government made it clear it wanted to retain exclusive access to personal and corporation income taxes. In exchange it offered to make substantial increases in existing grants to the provinces. With regard to health insurance, the government proposed contributions of approximately 60 percent of the cost of each provincial program introduced. There were many details but these three items made up the main thrust of the federal offer. Provincial officials returned home to give the proposals further study and within five months the disappointing returns began to come in. Most provinces supported early introduction of health insurance grants (and other social security measures that were part of the federal package), but it proved impossible for Ontario and Quebec to get past the taxation issues. Ontario Premier George Drew argued that abandoning direct taxation would place provinces in a "legislative strait-jacket":

> If the provincial governments placed themselves in such a position that they were only able to expand their activity with the approval of the Dominion Government, they would become little more than local administrative commissions of the Dominion Government…The steady whittling down of provincial rights of taxation would produce a limitation of legislative independence which could only have the effect of rapidly increasing the centralized power of the Dominion Government.

Personal and corporate income taxes must be returned to the provinces and, in addition, the federal government must withdraw from several other tax fields.

Premier Maurice Duplessis of Quebec was just as opposed. The federal financial proposals, he contended:

> …[T]end to replace the system of fiscal autonomy of the provinces in the field of taxation with a system of grants which would allow the Dominion government to exercise over them a financial tutelage control. Such a system is incompatible with their sovereignty.

After much scrambling for solutions by federal officials, a counteroffer was made to withdraw from one or two smaller tax fields and to increase grants to the provinces even further in exchange for retaining income tax rights. But a further counter-offer by Premier Drew brought negotiations to an end — Ontario was prepared to vacate and *rent* the income tax field to the federal government for an annual cash payment. Federal financial experts quickly produced calculations based on Drew's formula and estimated an additional federal obligation of almost $200 million over the original proposal. It was unacceptable, almost undo-able. With the end of negotiations, plans for health insurance and other social security measures were shelved.

●●●

To trace the true beginning of Canada's now famous health care system, the story jumps from the power struggles between Ontario, Quebec, and the central government to the independent action of the much less powerful province of Saskatchewan. Just as with workmen's compensation in Alberta and mothers' pensions in Manitoba, health insurance was introduced first in a part of Canada where public support, for one reason or another, was in advance of public support in other parts and certainly in advance of government action.

The history of the cooperative movement in Saskatchewan is now well-known. It developed out of necessity on an agricultural prairie where dependence on weather and soil conditions made for an uneven economy. Saskatchewan's population learned to live with such risks, but not without creating solutions to spread them more evenly. Cooperative action in marketing crops was the most widely-known innovation of Saskatchewan farmers, but cooperative systems of medical care had also been introduced in rural areas as early as World War I.[5] In a most straightforward solution to the problem of attracting doctors into isolated areas of the Prairies, local municipal councils simply offered to pay them a salary out of property tax revenues. This practice came later to include a personal tax on non-property owners as well. The provincial government struggled to keep abreast of these developments with many legislative changes to make it all legal.

Residents of Saskatchewan had also cooperated over the past

three decades in building local hospitals out of municipal tax revenues. By the early 1940s, 26 "union hospital districts" had been created and hospitals had been established to serve the residents of the towns, villages, and rural municipalities making up each district. Municipal revenues were also used to provide free hospital care for the needy and, in some cases, property tax revenues covered hospital bills for all ratepayers regardless of income. By 1942 almost 90 municipalities provided hospital services to their residents at municipal expense, some levying personal as well as property taxes.

Of all the provinces Saskatchewan had suffered most during the Depression and by far the largest burden of providing relief had fallen on the municipalities. In the 1940s the cooperative hospital and local doctor solutions they had introduced were growing beyond their fiscal means. Under pressure from municipalities and the strengthening CCF (which was the official opposition through two elections), the provincial government appointed a committee in 1943 to study the need for both social security and health services. Despite enthusiastic public response during its hearings, the committee moved slowly, waiting for federal action on the Marsh report health proposals which had been announced in the spring. Finally, with a provincial election approaching, the committee decided to act. In 1944 a Bill Respecting Health Insurance was passed, but it was then too late. Within two months the government was defeated, and health insurance became the responsibility of a new CCF administration.

The new government made several early decisions. The municipal doctor system had proved itself and would stay in effect for the time being with provincial subsidy for the first time. Priority in the development of a comprehensive health plan would be given instead to compulsory *hospital* insurance, the first stage and one that would cover all residents of Saskatchewan. Planning proceeded without delay. By the time the federal government called the doomed dominion-provincial conference in the late summer of 1945, Saskatchewan was already developing health regions throughout the province in preparation for hospital insurance. It was clear it would desperately need the 60 percent subsidy offered in the federal health proposals, but waiting was out of the question. As the conference in Ottawa stumbled through the power dynamics of the fall and early winter, Saskatchewan decided to go it alone. Its own legislation was being drafted and polished as Premier Duplessis of Quebec lectured federal officials at the conference about "tutelage control" and "sovereignty" and as Premier Drew of Ontario sharpened his pencil and demanded cash payments for "rental" of rights to tax his constituents. By late spring the Saskatchewan health bill was passed, and the following year the first government hospital insurance program in Canada was launched. The door on 60 percent funding had been closed in Ottawa. Saskatchewan would wait another 10 years for federal action.

By the end of the decade British Columbia and Alberta had both introduced similar programs.

•••

Fifty years had passed since Canadians first showed their opposition to any government offer of a helping hand to those in need. Lack of initiative and intemperance would be sure to follow such generosity. Now at mid-century there was strong public support for state involvement in social programs. Increasingly public opinion polls became a more scientific way of determining the attitudes and values of Canadian society than relying on newspaper editorials to interpret them. Newspapers, at best, fell short of objectivity when they were clearly aligned with one political party or another, and one had to read a broad cross-section of the press to draw any valid conclusions. Even after the federal government shelved the 1945 health proposals, pushing them off the front (and finally back) pages of newspapers across the country, a Gallup poll showed five years later that 80 percent of Canadians favoured a government health insurance program. Gallup polls of 1947, 1948, and 1950 also found that 90 percent of Canadians believed the family allowances program was "a good thing." This finding was reported as one of the largest majorities ever registered on national or international issues.

New programs would follow one after the other, and Canada would gain an international reputation as the best place to live. At mid-century the direction was unmistakably forward.

CHAPTER 6

Birth Pains of National Health Care

In the story of Canadian social legislation over the century, the 1950s and 1960s furnish most of the action. The two major programs — national health care and the national pension system — were constructed in stages, appearing at times like partly finished buildings waiting for further financing. And some would say the analogy is not inappropriate. With its foundation already in place in Saskatchewan, the national health care story is first. It provides all the elements of federal-provincial and interest-group politics that often delay or move along a program that has already won general public support.

When Saskatchewan decided to go it alone with its hospital insurance legislation in 1946, it had every reason to believe federal assistance would not be far off. The sometimes bitter exchange of tax proposals between Ottawa, Ontario, and Quebec was still in progress, and there was some hope the federal offer of health insurance funding would stand on its own regardless of the outcome of other financial negotiations. Instead, when negotiations failed, the federal government took its ball and went home. When Mackenzie King resigned as prime minister in 1948, he could look back on a satisfying record of achievement in social security — old age pensions for the poor, unemployment insurance and family allowances for all income groups — but a national health insurance plan had eluded him. It was true a system of national grants for health surveys had been introduced in 1948, but the issue of insurance was almost dead at the federal level. Nor did the new prime minister,

Louis St. Laurent, seem keen on reviving it. In the 1949 election campaign it received little mention.

As if to deal the final death blow, the Canadian Medical Association suddenly announced its opposition to a government-sponsored health plan. Earlier, when the 1945 health proposals were being drawn up, the CMA had been in total support and had even helped in designing the draft legislation. In the intervening years, however, hospitals and the medical profession had created their own solution — a system of voluntary prepaid hospital insurance which had become increasingly popular. This was of their own making, with their own rules. It served hospital and physician needs as well as the needs of patients who could afford insurance premiums. Not surprisingly, the uncertainties of the shape a government-sponsored plan would take were not attractive. Commercial insurers had also entered the hospital insurance field, and a predictable debate followed about the relative merits of free enterprise versus state programs. (This debate would take place again when the government announced Canada Pension legislation in the 1960s.)

At a dominion-provincial conference in 1950 Prime Minister St. Laurent shut the door on any hope for federal involvement in health insurance, though by now both Saskatchewan and B.C. were operating their own plans without assistance. According to the prime minister, defence expenditures related to the Korean War were as much as the federal government could handle. There was also the expense of old age pension improvements promised in the throne speech. Recent response from the provinces in making their health survey reports (under the National Health Grants program) also made it easier to place the health care plan on hold. Only two, Alberta and Saskatchewan, proposed state insurance plans in their reports. B.C., with its own plan in operation, did not propose a federal plan without further study. The rest of the provinces supported the use of non-government voluntary plans or simply documented the need for more hospital beds before insurance plans could even be considered. Not entirely unhappy with this mixed response, the prime minister seized on the issue of bed shortages and used it more than once to explain government inaction on health insurance.

Although the federal government and most of the provinces

showed little interest in a national health plan in 1950, a Gallup poll conducted the year before had revealed that 80 percent of Canadians approved of the idea. This was a rather remarkable denial of public opinion by both levels of government. In the House of Commons CCF member Stanley Knowles asked on 12 occasions over the next two years for the appointment of a committee to study the health insurance issue. Yet despite this political pressure and evident public support, there was no action.

The explanation lies partly in the fact that interest groups were now more actively taking the other side. The voluntary plans sponsored by hospitals and the medical profession had expanded dramatically between 1950 and 1952 (an increase of 43 percent in numbers enrolled), and commercial plans were also doing well. These developments prompted the Canadian Medical Association to reaffirm publicly the position it took in 1949 — the government should leave the health insurance field to the private sector. The Canadian Hospital Association and the Canadian Life Insurance Officers' Association soon added their support to the use of non-government plans. And with the injection of the private-versus-public element into the debate, the Canadian Chamber of Commerce followed suit. Who should provide the insurance became the focus of debate, not the issue of whether it should be provided at all. It had become obvious from the way the Canadian public had embraced the insurance principle by enrolling in voluntary plans that health insurance itself was not in question.

In the 1953 federal election campaign those in favour of government health insurance had a disappointing champion for their cause. George Drew, by then leader of the federal Progressive Conservatives, promised support of a national health insurance system that used voluntary and commercial plans. CCF leader J.W. Coldwell promised an immediate compulsory government plan. But St. Laurent made no promises. The official party statement was hardly electrifying:

> The Liberal party is committed to support a policy of contributory health insurance to be administered by the provinces when most of the provinces are ready to join in a nationwide scheme...

During the campaign opposition parties hammered away at the government for its failure to bring in health insurance. Drew insisted he could cut taxes by half a billion dollars and still bring in a national health program. Running for the fourth time, Knowles went after the government on behalf of the CCF: "They haven't announced anything. All you are asked to do is vote for Uncle Louie who seems to have become everybody's grandfather."

The Toronto *Globe and Mail*, supporting the Progressive Conservatives, criticized St. Laurent's inaction: "For years his Welfare Minister has been trolling around the country at public expense preaching a program of national health insurance."

The Canadian Medical Association also had its say. The main fear in connection with a federal health program, it contended many times during the campaign, was that it could be the first step toward state medicine.

In the end the Liberals were returned to office, but it would be a stretch of the imagination to attribute their victory in any way to their stand on national health insurance. Stanley Knowles again asked for a parliamentary committee on the subject and again was told that a committee would not be appointed. The tally was still two provinces, Saskatchewan and Alberta, with a commitment to a national plan. The federal government could delay without provincial criticism, and it did.

The impasse was finally broken in 1955 when Ontario, having shown no previous interest in a national health plan, began to take up the federal offer. If Ontario became the third province to make a commitment, three more might be encouraged to follow, adding up to the requirement laid down by Ottawa that *most* provinces must be ready to join. Given his lukewarm support of a new program, one can only speculate how this development was received by St. Laurent who otherwise, except for pressures from Knowles and some of his own cabinet, was quite comfortable leaving national health insurance to fade away.

The change of heart in Ontario was due to several unrelated factors. George Drew, having moved on to become leader of the national Progressive Conservatives, was replaced by Leslie Frost as premier. It is an understatement to describe the two men as dissimilar in personality. No less firm in his convictions, Frost was more inclined to go around rather than roll over his opponents. There could be more reasoned discussion, fewer ultimatums. He headed a province where almost two-thirds of the population was covered by voluntary or commercial hospital insurance plans. As a result, awareness of hospital insurance had been raised, and public debate was taking place on a subject that a decade before would not have stirred anyone. Opposition parties had campaigned vigorously about a health plan during the 1951 provincial election. And with a federal offer on the table, there was the usual pressure on any provincial government to utilize federal funding that was available.

The stumbling block was that the words *when most of the provinces are ready* seemed etched in granite. Pushed by Premier Frost to reopen the subject of national health insurance, Prime Minister St. Laurent repeated the offer of federal assistance, changing the requirement to *a substantial majority* of committed provinces. This clarification, intended to be conciliatory, only clouded the issue. But by now Frost was clearly aware of the level of public opinion in Ontario. He had been looking for an offer of funding for Ontario even if a majority of provinces refused to participate, and he was running out of time. The *Toronto Star*, among others, prodded him:

> The Prime Minister says Ottawa will finance in two stages — diagnostic services and then universal hospital insurance. That offer clearly puts the onus on the provinces and particularly on Ontario to clear the way for an early start on health insurance…If Mr. Frost means business on health insurance, the next move is up to him.

Still, throughout 1956 Ontario failed to make a commitment. For its part, the federal government failed to introduce legislation because a majority of provinces had not declared an interest, a decision that resulted in considerable public criticism at a time when a federal election within the year seemed a strong possibility. In the House there was further criticism. Stanley Knowles, after asking about a promised increase to old age pensions, observed:

> It is also highly noticeable, as my leader and others have pointed out, that there is no reference in the Speech from

the Throne to the question of health insurance...It begins to look as though the plan is virtually dead.

With public pressure on both governments, it became a question of which leader was the more anxious to have an Ontario plan, the premier of Ontario or the prime minister of Canada. The plan Ontario had designed was unique. It was to be voluntary, though Frost was certain enrolment would grow to 85 percent within a reasonably short time. This, he contended, should fulfill the "universal coverage" requirement for federal funding. But he had been overly optimistic about federal acceptance of his interpretation, and negotiations about universal coverage came to be crucial. The exchange of letters between Frost and St. Laurent illustrates the quiet, reasoned tone of these two men who were intent on finding a solution in which everyone would win. In reply to a letter from Frost which gave his estimate of 85 to 90 percent enrolment within a reasonable time, St. Laurent stated:

> We are of the opinion that, provided the estimates of coverage given in your letter are in fact realized when the proposed scheme becomes effective, it could properly be considered as coming within the framework of the federal government's proposals...

But 85 percent enrolment within a reasonable time did not mean *when the proposed scheme becomes effective*, and Frost could not make his plan work without federal funding during the start-up period, nor did he want to guarantee when the 85 percent figure would be reached. He replied:

> If this paragraph means that there would be no federal participation in our plan until we have reached 85 or 90 percent coverage, then it would seem to be a rejection of our proposal...We can achieve our objective of 85 to 90 percent, and perhaps more, provided we do it in a sound way. It is the judgment of the Government and its advisors here, it is upon sound, orderly administration that the success of this plan depends.

And from St. Laurent in reply:

> In regard to the coverage of your plan, the federal govern-
> ment has no desire that the government of Ontario should
> enter into any plan or undertaking which is unwise or
> impractical…We believe that if you feel that you should
> not give assurance of being able to reach your figure of
> 85% by a certain stage, it should be clearly set forth in our
> agreement that your plan will be universally available in
> fact as well as law and that your Commission will work
> without delay to obtain reasonably universal coverage.

Frost replied that the Hospital Services Commission would indeed
work without delay to obtain as wide coverage as possible. It was
not a new concession. Earlier in negotiations Frost had stayed away
from guarantees about the timing of universal coverage and now he
was adding nothing except a promise of diligent effort. But it was
enough. St. Laurent wrote back:

> I welcome the assurances you give in your letter concern-
> ing the policy that your Hospital Committee will follow in
> regard to coverage…I would suggest that as soon as they
> are ready, your Minister and officials most directly con-
> cerned with the programme might meet with Mr. Martin
> and our officials to draft agreement for federal support of
> it. I have no doubt that such discussion in detail will lead in
> due course to a form of agreement that will be satisfactory
> to both our governments.

And so the period of federal inaction was over. The correspondence between Frost and St. Laurent took place in the winter of
1957, and in March the minister of health and welfare, Paul Martin, introduced hospital insurance legislation in the House of Commons. In the House there were demands for removal of the six-
provinces requirement. Despite this and other objections, the Hospital Insurance and Diagnostic Services Act received unanimous
approval on third reading. Though the requirement for six provinces was never formally dropped, only five — Newfoundland,

Manitoba, Saskatchewan, Alberta, and B.C. — had programs in operation by July 1958 when the federal program became effective. Ontario, Nova Scotia, and New Brunswick had programs ready by the beginning of 1959 (at which time, incidentally, Ontario's enrolment was 92 percent). By 1961 almost the total population of Canada was entitled to hospital care benefits.

For residents of Saskatchewan and B.C. hospital benefits had been available for over 10 years. Indeed, Saskatchewan was ready to take the next step. With the federal contribution to hospital insurance, it could now proceed with a medical care insurance plan to cover the cost of physician services for all residents of Saskatchewan.

●●●

The health care story returns to Saskatchewan, but sadly it lacks the aura of goodwill and unity of purpose that characterized the pioneering efforts of the 1940s. The same government that had consulted and cooperated with the medical profession in the design of Canada's first hospital insurance legislation in 1946 began planning its medical care insurance in 1959 by making some important mistakes. Incredibly, in retrospect, it plunged ahead with six months of government planning without advising or consulting with the Saskatchewan College of Physicians and Surgeons (which also embodied the Saskatchewan Medical Association).

In the intervening 13 years new developments had brought changes to the health planning environment that partly explain this ultimately disastrous first step. The rapid expansion of profession-sponsored prepayment plans has been mentioned in the story of national hospital insurance. In Saskatchewan these voluntary plans covered approximately 40 percent of the population. Commercial insurance had also grown dramatically during the same period. Completely reversing their position of the 1940s, doctors in Saskatchewan, following the lead of the Canadian Medical Association, were now on record as opposing any medical services insurance plan that left out their own voluntary plans.

During the 13 years doctors had also learned what they could accomplish when they flexed their collective muscle. Opposed to a

1955 government plan to set up two regional medicare programs (in which a combination of prepaid premiums and taxes would cover the cost of physicians' services in a given region), doctors across the province had mobilized. Combining forces with the two major profession-sponsored health plans, they moved into the two health regions where referenda were to be held, made public speeches, put pressure on municipal leaders, and successfully defeated the government in each referendum.

Now in 1959, outraged and threatened by the government's failure to consult about the proposed medicare plan, doctors made a firm commitment to thwart its implementation. At the end of the ill-considered initial planning period, the government invited the medical profession to appoint representatives to a committee which would advise on the final design of the legislation. The doctors refused, then reconsidered and named three representatives who by one means or another managed to delay the work of the committee for several months over the next year.

During the period of the committee's work Saskatchewan doctors also actively opposed the government's medicare program in the provincial election, assessing each member of the association $100 to cover the publicity campaign. At every opportunity they promoted a medical services insurance system for Saskatchewan that would use their own voluntary insurance plans with government subsidy of low-income earners. Despite their efforts, however, the CCF party was returned to office.

Following the election the government's frustration with delays in the work of the advisory committee propelled it into its second mistake. The premier demanded an interim report from the committee and, based on the report, introduced medicare legislation almost immediately. The new act passed quickly through the Legislature without the input of the already hostile College of Physicians and Surgeons. Not surprisingly, when the Medical Care Insurance Commission was set up to administer the program, the doctors refused to participate by appointing representatives.

In the months that followed, the College of Physicians and Surgeons also refused several offers to meet with the minister of health to discuss possible amendments to the act. The college wanted the act repealed and nothing less. Finally the government made a surprising offer. Changes might be made which would allow doctors to practice outside the act — that is, they would bill and receive payment from their patients who would then apply for reimbursement from the provincial medicare plan. Given the potential for extra billing in this method, it was a major concession by the government. But there was no role for the doctors' voluntary insurance plans, and the offer was rejected.

With the starting date of the new medicare plan approaching, Saskatchewan doctors gave notice that they would withdraw normal medical services if it went into operation. Throughout the province their announcement was received with unexpected outrage directed mainly at the government. Citizens staged motorcades through the capital and demonstrations at the Legislature. Members of the opposition parties joined the battle. Along with doctors and leaders of the business community, they helped with organization and publicity. The quiet, uneventful city of Regina became a circus.

In the face of a threatened strike, the beleaguered government made arrangements to airlift doctors from Britain to provide services in distant outposts of the province as well as in the two major cities of Regina and Saskatoon. Undaunted, the doctors went on strike on July 1, 1962. Never would their public image completely recover from the damage of the next three weeks.

Within the borders of Saskatchewan the press was unanimously in support of the doctors. Most local newspapers interpreted the main issue as loss of freedom — "limitation of the rights of the individual and the community"; "democracy transformed into a dictatorship"; a "totalitarian" health commission, were a few of the comments. But outside the province the Canadian press generally condemned Saskatchewan doctors for deliberate defiance of a duly enacted law and for betrayal of the high ideals of their profession. The strike was also debated in the foreign press where, to an even greater degree, opinion was strongly against the unprofessional conduct of the doctors.

Finally the striking doctors agreed to talk to an intermediary suggested by the government and informally approved by the Canadian Medical Association. A member of the British House of Lords and a practising doctor, Lord Stephen Taylor, arrived on the scene and managed to gain the confidence of members of the Saskatchewan College of Physicians and Surgeons even though he had flown from Britain at the expense of the government. (Refusing a fee, he had agreed to help on condition that the government provide a week's fishing at the end of the informal negotiations.)

One of Lord Taylor's first decisions was that, given the high level of distrust and the potential for misunderstandings, representatives of the doctors and the government must be kept apart until agreement was reached. For eight days he walked back and forth between the headquarters of the College of Physicians and Surgeons in Saskatoon and the hotel where cabinet members were staying, three blocks away. The breakthrough came when the government made an offer to allow doctors to practise in association with any one of the voluntary insurance plans. As in the past they would submit bills to their chosen voluntary plan, but in future the voluntary plan would forward those bills to the government's medicare commission for payment. It was a circuitous route for the payment process but one that left the doctors a continuing (on the surface) relationship with their voluntary plans and a non-recognition (again on the surface) of a government payment system. For their part, the doctors agreed that the medicare plan would be universal and compulsory.

The strike ended with the signing of an agreement based on these two concessions. It had been a costly episode for the medical profession. Saskatchewan lost 68 doctors in 1962, although by the middle of 1964 the total complement of doctors in the province had increased to its highest level. There could be no precise measure of what they had lost in prestige in the tragic events of 1962. At the outset of the plan most doctors chose to take up the option of billing their own voluntary plans and waiting while the bills went to the commission and back; only 21 percent chose to bill the medicare commission directly. Over time this situation was reversed. By 1970 over 51 percent of doctors were billing the commission directly.

Although the fireworks were over in Saskatchewan, there were more to come at the federal level. Voluntary plans in the first province to introduce medicare had been reduced to the role of billing and payment conduits. Still, the Saskatchewan experience only strengthened the resolve of the Canadian Medical Association and the voluntary plans it sponsored across the country. As a result of their combined efforts, the next three provinces that began to plan their own medicare programs followed CMA recommendations for a non-compulsory program in which individuals who could afford premiums were free to enrol in voluntary plans, while those who could not were subsidized by the government. By the time the federal government began to talk about national medicare, Alberta and B.C. had brought in legislation along these lines and Ontario was moving in the same direction.

In June 1964 the CMA and its voluntary plans were jolted by an unexpected setback. The Royal Commission on Health Services, set up three years earlier by the previous Conservative government, presented its final report and recommended a national medicare system in which the federal government would assist provinces with medicare programs that offered uniform terms and conditions to the entire population. It was clear the recommendation for uniform conditions ruled out the CMA model of subsidizing low-income earners (who would necessarily be required to pass a means test). The royal commission report only served to step up CMA efforts to hold the federal government to a voluntary program for most of the population and the subsidization of some.

At the same time the government had other challenges to consider besides the CMA. As it prepared its proposal for a national medicare program, it was well aware that provincial attitudes toward cost-shared programs had changed dramatically since the hospital insurance agreements signed between 1958 and 1960. Provinces were no longer willing to enter into agreements that came with federally imposed requirements and federal audits. It was a new era of provincial autonomy. With this in mind the federal government proposed a fiscal contribution to each provincial medicare program rather than a conditional grant, limiting requirements to five criteria: provincial plans must be comprehensive (all medically necessary services provided by both general practitioners and specialists), universal (covering all residents on uniform terms and conditions), publicly administered, reasonably accessible, and portable (fully transferable from one province to another). For provinces with programs meeting these criteria, Ottawa would pay half the average per capita cost of providing medical services.

Two of these criteria caused problems for Alberta, B.C., and Ontario. Using voluntary insurance plans, their existing or planned medicare programs were neither universal nor totally publicly administered. The CMA, whose pressure had influenced the design of these three programs, was also clearly against the government proposal. Although legislation was introduced before the summer recess of 1966, the provinces and the CMA used the recess to mount a more vocal campaign of opposition. The government had to weigh this opposition against public opinion polls which were showing 82 percent of Canadians were convinced that a satisfactory plan of medicare could be worked out to meet everyone's needs.

But opposition was not all external to the government. A division in the cabinet also threatened the medicare plan, especially the resistance of the finance minister, Mitchell Sharp. He warned higher taxes would be needed to pay for the cost of medicare and he wanted the plan delayed. Former Health Minister Judy LaMarsh, however, charged that Sharp had intentionally allied himself with CMA and provincial opposition to gain support for his candidacy in a possible Liberal leadership race. The conflict seemed beyond resolution, even though polls were showing 74 percent of Canadians still wanted medicare even if it meant higher taxes. In the end, both internal and external opposition maintained pressure on the government as the medicare bill went through second and third readings and the program's starting date was delayed a year.

During the House debate, Davie Fulton, member of the Conservative opposition, sharply criticized the government's requirement for a publicly administered program:

> On the basis of the minister's proposal, all private plans must be wiped out and this plan must be publicly administered. Let me ask him and the committee what is going to happen to some of the very adequate and excellent private plans now in existence...?

When the Conservatives introduced an amendment to delay the government's bill still further, a member of Parliament commented to the House:

It looks as though neither of these parties is willing to face private insurance companies and give the Canadian people any real social progress.

Still another, after praising the minister of health and welfare's leadership in the spring in bringing the bill forward, went on:

> ….[T]his fall we saw that minister crumble under the pressure of the Minister of Finance who had emerged as a power with the backing of the big, vested financial, insurance and professional interests in this country which do not want medicare now nor for a long time to come.

Though the minister appeared to be crumbling, he was successful in steering medicare through to its final passage without compromising any of the five federal principles.

When the national medicare program began in 1968, Saskatchewan and B.C. qualified for the federal contribution. By the following year the plans of Newfoundland, Nova Scotia, Manitoba, Alberta, and Ontario were in operation. Quebec and P.E.I. followed in 1970 and New Brunswick in 1971. Within a few years the federal government found that the fiscal contribution method introduced for medicare did 'not allow a reasonable control on its own expenditures. Within 10 years it replaced the funding arrangements of all health agreements with a transfer of income tax points and payments to the provinces that were related to the gross national product.

CHAPTER 7

Support and Snags on the Way to National Pensions

Throughout the 1950s and 1960s the development of Canada's national pension system ran alongside the development of its health care system. With public opinion by then more generally in sympathy with the insecurities faced by industrial workers,[6] successive federal governments of both major parties added pensions to their policy agendas during the two decades. But concern for workers was not the only reason. The new interest in pensions was also related to the government's traditional role in overseeing the economic activities of the nation.

Fair or not, governments are judged by the health of the economy. Voters throw them out when profits are low or jobs are scarce or prices are high. Governments are even in trouble when crops are poor and fish in short supply. It is almost universally understood that one of the government's main functions is to maintain conditions throughout the country that will allow the economy to thrive. To this end, concessions like tax exemptions and tough labour laws are made to the business sector; unemployment insurance and more permissive labour laws are conceded to workers; subsidies are granted to farmers; and so on.

Political scientists argue that social security measures like unemployment insurance and pensions are not exclusively concessions to workers. Contrary to conventional wisdom, they may provide benefits to business as well. For example, they may dispel labour unrest, or to emphasize the positive, social security measures can help create an atmosphere of industrial harmony that makes it possible to conduct business and maintain profits without disruption.

If this is so, some social programs will have easier passage through the legislative process than others. Broad public opinion may support a measure that would help the ordinary Canadian, but its success and timing could depend on whether or not business believes it is absolutely necessary for industrial harmony. In the early part of the century business resistance to workmen's compensation was well-documented, but when employers finally recognized the advantages of reduced labour tension in a workplace free of litigation, resistance turned to support. In the 1930s business contended that relief payments were the worst kind of paternalism, but when the unemployed began to disrupt employment offices and organize marches on Ottawa, opposition faded away. And though relief was finally acceptable as an emergency measure, many attributed the long delays in bringing in unemployment insurance to pressure on Prime Minister King from the business community which was not ready for such a permanent solution. Only when King believed public opinion was stronger than the resistance of business was he willing to act.

At mid-century there was less outspoken criticism from business. Its leaders had learned to mind their manners and speak in euphemisms. Public relations and corporate advertising became popular; employees were part of the corporate family in which everyone cared for everyone else. ("NOFALCO isn't just a place to work — it's a way of life," claimed the ads.) It helped that after a few years of postwar sluggishness the economy recovered and business could afford to be less grumpy. The first social program to appear in the new half-century was a universal program of old age pensions. It had been shelved along with other proposals when the 1945 Dominion-Provincial Conference on Reconstruction failed. Now it became the pet of business and nothing could stop it.

Labour activities in the immediate postwar period in both the U.S. and Canada explain this turn of events. With wartime wage ceilings still in effect, labour had simply replaced its demands for wage increases with demands for fringe benefits and, among benefits, pension plans were highest on the most-wanted list. The first action took place in the U.S. From 1946 when the first negotiated pension plan was won by the United Mine Workers, American trade unions conducted a relentless drive for pensions over the next five years, chiefly directed at the coal, steel, and automobile industries. In 1949 American steelworkers went out on strike over the issue. Within a month 37 basic steel companies agreed to provide pension plans for their workers. In the same year, without having to strike, the United Automobile Workers (UAW) settled a pension plan agreement with Ford. Chrysler was also in the midst of lengthy negotiations on the issue of pensions.

By 1949 Canadian industry was under the same pressure. Striking asbestos miners in Quebec included a pension plan in their demands; lithographers on strike in Ontario and goldminers in B.C. made the same demands. At the same time UAW workers at Ford of Canada, following their American counterparts, were negotiating a pension agreement. When the matter was concluded after many months, the *Globe and Mail* gave front-page coverage, calling it the "first major union-negotiated pension settlement in Canada." Ontario clothing workers followed within a week with a settlement for a plan involving 3,500 workers.

It was not long before the business sector in Canada began a campaign of doom. Pensions were about to create as heavy a financial burden on industry as wages. Articles began to appear in *Canadian Business* and *Industrial Canada*, periodicals that reached a wide audience of fellow-sufferers. One article claimed that industry had almost reached its capacity to absorb further pension costs and still operate profitably. Another argued that government must help. The problem was unique to Canada, it was claimed, because the U.S. government's social security system already provided a basic pension to all retired Americans. As a result, in their labour negotiations U.S. industries were able to offer lower pensions which simply topped up the social security flat-rate amount.

In Canada there was no counterpart to the basic pension offered by U.S. social security. The old age pension program of the Canadian government reached only a few — those who successfully passed a means test. Over the years there had been much dissatisfaction about the stringent nature of the test. Pensioners had to remain virtually destitute to qualify. In some cases, they were still hounded after their death when the government made claims on their estates. Labour and the general public wanted the despised means test removed.

Threatened with new and substantial costs related to their own negotiated pensions, business and industrial leaders now threw in their support for the removal of the means test from government pensions and the introduction of a pension system for all workers. The more Ottawa pays, the *Financial Post* explained to any of its readers who might still wonder whether the world had gone crazy, the less will be demanded of industry. The *Canadian Banker* also felt the need to explain the sudden enthusiasm of employers for a new old age pension system. But the most telling media contribution was a news story in the *Globe and Mail*. Management officials of Ford of Canada, it was reported, had recently travelled to Ottawa (as part of a joint delegation that included UAW representatives with whom they were negotiating) for an interview with Health and Welfare Minister Paul Martin. The purpose of the interview, the *Globe and Mail* learned, was to press the minister to move forward with a universal pension.

Martin denied publicly that any such commitment had been made. A few days later, however, he announced the creation of a joint Senate-House committee on old age pensions. Commenting on the announcement, one member of Parliament observed wryly: "We find ourselves in the position where industrialists and financiers are [now] advocating the taking away of the means test." In a supporting address another member reported that one of Canada's largest manufacturers, based in his constituency, had recently written him with a strong recommendation for a universal pension system. When the joint Senate-House committee began its hearings, there was further support from the Canadian Chamber of Commerce and the Canadian Manufacturers' Association, both traditional foes of social security measures.

While the business community may have played an uncharacteristic role in supporting legislation aimed at helping workers, it clearly wanted workers to contribute to the proposed pensions. Recommendations for a universal system were simply recommendations to eliminate the means test and make pensions available to all workers over the age of 70. But the method of financing such a system was a separate issue. In its presentations to the joint committee and in all its public statements the business community favoured a social insurance plan with payroll contributions similar to those for unemployment insurance. In such plans contributions and benefits were not pegged at a flat rate but instead were wage-related. The government, however, seemed unable to meet both the demands of time and the demands of a complex administrative scheme, and in the end it opted for a flat-rate plan available to all Canadians over 70 without compulsory contributions. Earmarked corporation, personal income and sales taxes were to be levied to cover the cost. While this decision was criticized both in the House and in the press ("We would not even venture to guess the real motives which fathered the scheme," said the *Globe and Mail* in exasperation), the government had managed to come up with a speedy solution that temporarily satisfied both business and labour.

But temporary it was. Organized labour kept up its pressure throughout the 1950s for a contributory wage-related pension plan that would compensate for the deficiencies that were now becoming evident in their negotiated industrial plans. Portability was one problem; another was inadequate coverage with only a third of the total Canadian labour force enrolled in industrial pension plans.

Besides labour, the general public supported more government action in social security and, in fact, expected it from either party in power. The Conservative government, in office from 1957 to 1963, brought in increases to old age pensions, moved ahead the starting date for hospital insurance, and set up the Royal Commission on Health Services. During the election campaign it had also promised a national pension system. When polled in 1960 about the "best thing" in the Conservative government's record over the past two years, Canadians mentioned these and other social welfare services more often than any other government action.

Five years in opposition, during which the Conservatives brought in these social measures and threatened more, gave the Liberal government a sense of urgency when it returned to office in April 1963. By June a resolution for a national pension system was before the House. Within a week, however, the first indication of trouble appeared. On the recommendation of a governmental committee, the Quebec National Assembly unexpectedly passed a resolution to stay out of any proposed federal plan. Instead Quebec would prefer to have its own plan, answering the specific needs of Quebecers. Most important, while the federal government envisioned a pay-as-you-go system of financing, Quebec was determined to have the opposite. Premier Jean Lesage announced that one of the features of a Quebec plan would be the development of a large public investment fund which would become an important instrument of Quebec's economic policy. In short, with a growing commitment to manage its own affairs, Quebec was threatening to opt out.

Within a month there was further bad news. Private insurance companies in Ontario came out strongly opposed to the federal plan and began to mobilize for action, a development that kept Premier John Robarts from giving his support to Ottawa's proposal. Canada's two largest provinces were poles apart. With frustration, Health and Welfare Minister Judy LaMarsh observed:

> Mr. Lesage's plan could finish the private insurance business in Quebec... Mr. Robarts would turn the whole insurance field over to the private insurance companies.

With trouble on two fronts the federal government first turned its attention to Ontario. Cabinet members, especially the health and welfare minister, promoted the federal pension plan with personal appearances and speeches in Ontario, notably during the provincial election campaign which started in late summer. But they were up against insurance companies that were determined to dump the plan. During the summer the vice-president of Canada Life addressed the Ontario Chamber of Commerce and warned its members of the serious consequences of a government contributory plan. In the fall the president of Great-West Life warned anyone who would listen that Canadians would become over-pensioned if the plan were put into operation. Interviewed by the *Globe and Mail*, he called on Canadian business to support "a militant campaign for a public probe of the proposed federal pension legislation." A Great-West Life pamphlet, *Let's Raise a Storm,* was widely circulated, urging business and financial institutions to step up political pressure. Letters of protest from the business community to the prime minister and members of cabinet followed in the wake of these calls for action. LaMarsh, who was still three years away from the campaign against medicare mounted by the private medical services industry, commented:

> You have seen some well-organized elections...but you have seen no better organized campaign than this insurance lobby. The private insurance companies have pledged that they will use all their resources against the plan. We have a veritable power-house against us.

It was remarkable that in a little over 10 years the business community had completely reversed its position on pensions. Where were the calls to bring in better pensions that had appeared in *Canadian Business* and *Industrial Canada* in 1950? Where were the earlier lobbying activities for government action in reducing poverty among older Canadians? They not only were missing in the 1960s, but had been replaced by demands that the government stay out of the pension business.

The reasons for this new position taken by the corporate world were not mysterious. In its proposed Canada Pension Plan (CPP) the government had finally moved from non-contributory flat-rate benefits as in the Old Age Security Act to a contributory wage-related plan. Aside from the requirement for payroll deductions, CPP pensions would come dangerously close to the pensions sold by life insurance companies and others in the private pension business.

Yet this similarity was nothing new. In the 1960s many could even recall that Canadian industry had actually preferred and promoted a contributory system 13 years earlier. In the interim, however, everything had changed. It was no longer Canadian industry that spoke out about pensions; it was those in the business of selling pensions, principally the insurance companies. When old age security legislation was introduced in 1951, the voice of the private pension industry had been absent, but only because there was no private pension industry of any size or importance.

The rapid growth of labour-negotiated pension plans following the 1950 Ford of Canada settlement continued throughout the decade, and there was no question insurance companies enjoyed a large share of a very profitable market. Pension fund assets in plans administered by insurance companies, trust companies, and the government grew from $869 million in 1952 to $2.6 billion in 1960. By the late 1950s trust companies, having made a late start in the pension field, had caught up to insurance companies in pension assets. In 1963 insurance companies were holding a slight edge, but the announcement of a government pension plan which would add yet another competitor was the final straw. When the insurance industry exploded into public view in June, their militancy surprised nearly everyone but the trust companies.

Confronted with this noisy campaign, Premier Robarts of Ontario decided that no action would be better than the wrong action. Though Ontario may have seen flaws in the federal proposal, the premier was not willing to be accused of lining up with the powerful pension industry. And so he waited, while federal officials grew more and more frustrated without the support of Canada's largest province for their proposed plan. Discussions with Ontario limped on through the fall and winter of 1963-64. At a federal-provincial conference in November, the federal government moved from its proposed pay-as-you-go design to a partially funded plan, with half of the funds to be turned over to the provinces. In light of this attractive financial offer, other provinces appeared to be warming to the new concept, but Ontario still held out.

The federal government introduced its pension bill in the House of Commons in March, confident the provinces would respond once legislation was in place. But the long-awaited action from Ontario dashed federal hopes. To everyone's horror, Premier Robarts announced that if Quebec was not willing to join the national plan, Ontario would consider having its own provincial plan as well.

The focus of federal strategy quickly turned from Ontario to Quebec. Federal officials had already seen the provisions of the proposed Quebec Pension Plan and knew that the federal plan offered less coverage and less generous benefits. The question was: How far could they move toward the Quebec design, still keep the support of the federal treasury, and not close the door on Ontario where the insurance industry was agitating for lower benefits?

The story of the Ottawa-Quebec negotiations that followed Ontario's announcement had "all the trimmings of plot and counterplot," according to one critical member of the opposition speaking in the House. Aware they had everything to lose without Quebec participation in a national pension plan, Prime Minister Lester B. Pearson and his chief aide, Tom Kent, were apparently willing to listen when Maurice Sauvé, a junior cabinet minister, urged private talks with Claude Morin, Quebec's deputy minister for federal-provincial affairs and also a personal friend. As Sauvé related to the *Montreal Star* later, he and Kent flew secretly to Quebec City, even taking the precaution of booking rooms at the Château Frontenac under assumed names.[7] They began negotiations with Claude Morin and within a few hours an initial agreement was reached that Ottawa would bring its pension plan more in line with Quebec's proposed design. The first concession made by Kent and Sauvé was a commitment to turn over 100 percent of the pension's funds to the provinces. The second was a suggestion that the federal government might give the provinces a greater share of income tax revenues.

Later in the same day the negotiating group slipped in the side entrance to Premier Lesage's office, outlined the main features of the proposal, and received the premier's tentative approval. Many details of the compromise plan would have to be negotiated but, for the time being, Lesage indicated that the two major federal concessions would be seriously considered by Quebec.

Still with great secrecy Kent and Sauvé then flew in a Quebec government aircraft to Ottawa where they went directly to the prime minister's residence at 24 Sussex and laid out the proposal to Pearson and key cabinet members. Not too unexpectedly, Finance Minister Walter Gordon had strong reservations about the new size and shape the Canada Pension Plan was beginning to take. With Pearson's support, however, negotiations continued with Quebec City.

Although access to CPP funds and new income tax revenues were major concessions, over the next few days the two sides ultimately reached an impasse over the details of the plan. Once again the federal negotiators saw a national plan slipping away. To head off disaster they proposed a compromise. Quebec and the federal government would each have its own pension plan, each with identical contributions and benefits, but fully coordinated. In addition, Quebec would be allowed to opt out of the federal family allowance program (an arrangement it had frequently demanded) in exchange for fiscal payments in an equivalent amount. And after further negotiations it could opt out of a wide range of shared-cost programs. All told, federal concessions were substantial, but the impasse was broken.

With the Quebec agreement in place, the federal government sought approval of the other provinces. It was many months before Ontario, still under pressure from the life insurance industry, finally gave its support. Rumour had it that it could not, after all, afford to operate an Ontario-only plan. And there was a strong sense that the fragile compromise reached between Ottawa and Quebec could not be jeopardized. Insurance companies felt abandoned by Ontario and by the federal government. Appearing before a joint Senate-House committee in early 1965, they again asked that the CPP be scrapped in favour of an amended Old Age Security Act. But the events of the past year had turned the tide against them. The CPP bill proceeded to the House where it finally passed after a lengthy debate.

Across the country the tone of newspaper editorials reflected the strain of the long-drawn-out struggle for a national pension system. The *Globe and Mail* described the final passage of the bill as "an historic event...perhaps the most important piece of legislation to go through the House of Commons since the Second World War." The *Victoria Times* claimed the government had "attained a major social objective and fashioned a charter for retirement security which will have a profoundly significant impact on Canadian society."

But not everyone agreed. The *Edmonton Journal* called the CPP "an unjustified intrusion by the state in the field of private responsibility and private rights." The *Halifax Chronicle* commented: "The plan has been called the most progressive legislation ever introduced in Canada; it has also been called the biggest boondoggle ever foisted on a bewildered people."

But the *Vancouver Province* neither criticized nor congratulated the government. It chose instead to congratulate Canadians themselves:

Passage of the Canada Pension Plan by the House of Commons is a significant milestone in the development of what is coming to be known as the nation's social consciousness... Forty years ago the idea of giving public money away in such quantities would have been considered revolutionary. That it is now so widely regarded as a natural social and economic step is a measure of the changing dimension of public thinking.

Three months later legislation covering the Quebec Pension Plan was passed in the National Assembly. Both plans, fully portable across the country, went into operation on January 1, 1966.

•••

In the 1960s one piece of social legislation followed another in rapid succession. The Canada Pension Plan received parliamentary approval in March 1965, the National Medical Care Insurance Act in December and the Guaranteed Income Supplement in 1966. There still remained the Canada Assistance Plan which was introduced in 1966, a mammoth program whose central feature was federal cost-sharing of provincial and municipal welfare, the old "relief" programs for the unemployed.

By the 1960s public relief, then known as public welfare, had not only changed its name, but had also been transformed. It had evolved from life in the poorhouse at the turn of the century, to outdoor relief or private charity hand-outs made after a good deal of inspection to ensure applicants were deserving, to municipal soup kitchens and breadlines during the Depression, and, as public attitudes changed, to payments of cash to the poor.

Unemployment insurance in 1941 was intended to shift the emphasis from the emergency nature of relief to the more methodical forward-looking insurance principle. While they were working, workers would make contributions to a fund which would provide for them in (the presumably rare) case of unemployment. The problem with the insurance principle was that benefits were limited to a specified number of weeks and, for many who could not find work, benefit periods ran out. Even in the best of times there was also a whole group of unemployed who had never made contributions because they had never worked — disabled or in poor health, such people were, in fact, unemployable. As a result, relief programs existed in some provinces and many municipalities long after the introduction of unemployment insurance and long after federal assistance to emergency relief had stopped.

In the early 1950s Ottawa agreed to help provincial governments with public welfare costs for the blind and disabled in financial need. Within a few years it also entered into agreements to cost-share welfare payments to the able-bodied unemployed. It was these separate agreements that were later rolled up into the Canada Assistance Plan in 1966. For the first time the federal government was offering to fund public welfare on a permanent rather than an emergency basis.

There was another first. With the introduction of the Canada Assistance Plan the federal government began to cost-share mothers' pensions, the provincial programs that had started out modestly during World War I and had come to represent the largest portion of welfare costs in every province. With marriage breakdown on the increase, the offer to cost-share mothers' pensions was a move filled with financial uncertainty. And how much public support the program enjoyed was an unknown factor.

After 50 years of mothers' pensions, public opinion was still divided on whether they were beneficial or harmful to single mothers, their children, and Canadian taxpayers. As well, the issue was clouded with the stirrings of the second wave of feminism in the century. Was the government actually providing these pensions to keep women out of the labour force? On the other hand, was it not right and proper for a mother to place her child-rearing responsibilities ahead of any goal she may have of improving the family's economic position? Still, what about the obligation of all parents to provide as best they can for their families rather than looking to the government for help? Canadians were still undecided about these issues.

For the federal government, which was about to provide funding for the first time, there was a simpler question: Why not get all these women to work (where many of them would prefer to be) and save millions of dollars in welfare costs? Federal policymakers quietly introduced a middle-of-the-road solution and buried it in the text of the Canada Assistance Plan. In future, single parents could choose to go to work over staying on welfare — the federal and provincial governments would subsidize their child care costs. Whether by design or not, this new "welfare service" appeared a minor part of the government's proposed assistance plan. Throughout the entire debate in the House it barely received a mention.

But federal child care funding turned out to be a rare instance of legislation put into place long before a good part of the public was ready for it. Though the issues had not been debated at the federal level (or, rather, were simply lost in the shuffle), they were still not resolved at the local level. The opposition to children being cared for outside the home was still a reality in many areas of Canada, especially if the community rather than the wider family circle was being asked to share the responsibility. A member of the Ontario Legislature summarized the prevailing philosophy:

> Aunts and grandparents are all right, and so is the dear family friend. Privately arranged, the fact of sharing the parental responsibility for the safety and wellbeing of small children is viewed as responsible. Sought from the community on the same basis, the very parent may find herself subjected to hostility, criticisms and accusations of parental irresponsibility.

This conflict of social values initially took its toll on the availability of child care services even with the new offer of funding under the Canada Assistance Plan. Local and provincial governments, reflecting the attitudes of local and provincial taxpayers, were often reluctant to introduce spending on child care even with a federal commitment to match it. And single mothers, an unorganized and isolated group, lacked the political power to make the case that more child care dollars would mean less welfare dollars.

By the late 1960s pressure for child care facilities began to develop out of the growing feminist movement. Middle-class mothers were going to work in increasing numbers and were willing to pay for good out-of-the-home child care. There was also support for more child care from the Royal Commission on the Status of

Women, which was set up in 1967 and reported in 1970. The Commission commented:

> The time is past when society can refuse to provide community child services in the hope of dissuading mothers from leaving their children and going to work.

Single mothers watched these new developments from the sidelines and reaped the benefits. Child care would turn out to be a major growth industry over the next decade as both single and married mothers went to work at a rate unprecedented in the century. Public attitudes also began to change. Over 93 percent of Canadians polled in 1960 thought married women with children should not take a job outside the home; 80 percent thought so in 1970, and 72 percent in 1975. And although almost three-quarters of Canadians wanted married women to stay home, 61 percent approved when the Royal Commission on the Status of Women recommended a national network of day nurseries.

While child care became an unexpectedly large line item in Canada Assistance Plan spending, the major portion of federal cost-sharing under the plan was directed at public welfare payments. These payments skyrocketed during the economic downturn of the 1970s, making the federal government question more than once the feasibility of continuing with a dollar-for-dollar formula.

CHAPTER 8

Deindexing, Dismantling, Devaluing

As Canadians approached the three-quarter mark in the century, they could take some pride in their national social programs: unemployment insurance for the jobless, pensions for the elderly, health care for the whole population, and public assistance for many disadvantaged people unable to provide for themselves. These programs were funded from a variety of sources — taxes, personal contributions, and employer contributions — and sometimes a combination of the three. Whatever the funding source, they reflected a Canadian philosophy, long in the making, that the healthy should be responsible for the sick and the fortunate for the unfortunate.

In embracing this philosophy Canada moved away from the North American worship of individualism which had held back collective solutions to problems of industrialization. Instead the extent of its social legislation began to move ever so slightly in the direction of Western European countries. In 1960, according to data collected by the Organization for Economic Cooperation and Development, Canada's social spending represented 12 percent of gross domestic product; in 1974 its social spending was over 20 percent of GDP. In these two years U.S. social expenditures as a percentage of GDP were 11 and 19 respectively, while corresponding European percentages were approximately 15 and 25.

In the early 1970s Canada continued to expand its social spending by increasing benefits in some existing programs. The Unemployment Insurance (UI) Act was amended to include new groups of workers, giving it almost universal coverage. In addition, the qualifying period for access to UI payments was shortened from seven months to eight weeks, and benefits were increased from 43 to 66 percent of earnings. The Family Allowances Act was also amended, almost tripling monthly benefits and including indexing for the first time.

Under the cost-sharing provisions of the Canada Assistance Plan, child care services continued to grow, the number of spaces increasing by almost 380 percent in the early 1970s (from 17,391 in 1972 to 83,520 in 1976). Provinces and municipalities also introduced or expanded many new services aimed at helping people to get off welfare, services such as counselling, homemaker services, rehabilitation, and others. Some services were even made available to the working poor.

But sadly the spirit of help and caring was coming to an end. Over the next 15 years Canadians watched (first with misgiving, then with wholehearted support) as their valued social programs became less valuable. As Canada and the world suffered a major economic crisis, periods of considerable restraint were followed by periods of severe restraint. Without question, the most vulnerable groups in Canadian society were the hardest hit and — reminiscent of attitudes in the early part of the century — few saw the need for collective solutions.

•••

Our sympathy and support for unemployed workers is a fragile thing. It tends to disappear when general unemployment is high, the very occasion when they need it most. Faced with large numbers out of work, we are all too eager to accept the suggestion that some of them really prefer to be unemployed. With the comfort we get from generalizations, we soon have it that not just some, but all, unemployed workers are enjoying their life of leisure.

Why this is so is at times beyond understanding. Does there lurk a human tendency to believe that our fellow man in need of help is really faking? We readily take as gospel the story of the street beggar in rags who really has thousands of dollars under his mattress at home. We nod without questioning when someone tells us that people who use handicapped parking spaces (though they may actually hobble away from the car in braces) are not really handicapped. We like to hear that charities campaigning for funds spend most of our donations on administration, especially if we can conjure up a high-paid executive going from home to charity office in a chauffeur-driven limousine.

This human tendency to doubt that need actually exists, to suspect that unemployed people could really be working but choose not to be, can be traced to human attitudes toward work itself. Meaningful work, it is true, provides a feeling of personal satisfaction and achievement that can rarely be gained from other activity. If all work was meaningful, it would rank high on everyone's list of how they would like to spend their waking hours. But for millions in society the type of work that must be undertaken to earn a living has little personal significance. In fact, the tasks involved in many jobs are so far removed from their final purpose that the resulting loss of control felt by workers has been described as "alienation." For centuries it has been necessary to use incentives of one kind or another to persuade people to take on such work.[8] As we have seen, even at the beginning of the 20th century vagrancy laws provided the incentive of punishment; moral and religious teachings provided the incentive of social isolation or stigmatism. Today downward adjustments to unemployment insurance benefits are intended to have a similar effect. The very existence of incentives is evidence that work is unpleasant. If we could maintain our standard of living and our freedom from social stigma, wouldn't we really prefer leisure ourselves? Small wonder that a history of suspicion surrounds our perception of the motives of unemployed workers.

The abandonment of the unemployed during sluggish economic periods stems from the same cynicism. The general public, fully aware of high national unemployment and a worldwide economic slowdown, can still believe that unemployment is caused by the unemployed. A form of selective vision, this inclination can be exploited and often is. Governments covering with smoke their own inadequate performances in providing stable economic conditions and business hoping to shift public attention from its reluctance to provide jobs when profits decline, like to suggest that unemployed workers are malingering. Who can argue with program cuts if they are aimed at reducing this vast number of idlers and layabouts? The story of Canada's unemployment insurance plan from the mid-1970s to the end of the century is the story of this decreasing generosity to Canadians who are out of work. Though public mistrust has been regularly nurtured by legislators and employers who seize every opportunity to blame unemployment on cheaters, the public itself has accepted this verdict without enough analysis.

By 1975 the unemployment rate had grown from an average of 4.2 percent in the late 1960s to 7.1 percent, making excessive demands on the unemployment insurance fund. Canada had come to the end of a 30-year period of steady economic growth and high employment. A world economic crisis caused by a combination of events — oil price increases, the oversupply of consumer goods, increased industrial competition from Japan and parts of Europe, inflation caused by the war in southeast Asia, technological advances — changed Canadian policies almost overnight. In June the federal government introduced an unemployment insurance bill cutting back some of the more generous qualifying periods and benefits legislated in 1971. Studies suggest, said Finance Minister John Turner, that "some features of the new [1971] system have undesirable effects on work incentives." So, 35 years after unemployment insurance was first implemented, the debate was to be reopened on whether a system in which workers insure themselves against loss of income would, in fact, destroy their incentive to work and lead them into a life of idleness.

Members of the opposition challenged the Liberal government on its sudden shift to stricter measures after years of championing the unemployment insurance program. One member quietly pointed out the irony of the government's new emphasis on the work ethic, quoting Prime Minister Pierre Elliot Trudeau in a 1972 interview with the *Edmonton Journal*:

I say that the most sacred law is that a man who lives in society should be able to enjoy his own possibilities to the maximum, but work is not the way to do it. If we are lucky, we will move toward a leisure society where we will work less. The aim of man in society is not to work, it is to realize his own potential to the maximum.

Though the government might have wished its prime minister had chosen to talk philosophy anywhere but in the down-to-earth province of Alberta (and perhaps perversely had chosen to do it there), the unemployment insurance bill continued its way through second and third readings in the House. The Conservative opposition supported it and, if anything, would have preferred stricter cutbacks.

Two years later, with unemployment at 8.6 percent, new legislation brought in still more drastic measures. The period of employment required for workers to qualify for UI was increased from eight to 12 weeks, a change that "would constitute for many of them an incentive to work longer," according to the government. On the third day of the House debate most newspapers in Canada carried a press release from the Unemployment Insurance Commission announcing that unemployment officials were clamping down on cheaters. The release went on to say that "overpayments amounted to only 1.86 percent of total benefits paid out in 1976, but the Commission is pressing forward with programs to uncover fraud."

It was clear the prime minister's philosophy of a "leisure society" had not filtered down to his own public service staff. Later in the week, when asked about the 50,000 claimants who were about to be cut off, a senior manpower official told the *Toronto Star*:

> They are mostly young people, moving in and out of the labour force and using unemployment insurance to fatten their income.

On the subject of providing benefits while workers took part in training programs, he commented: "It's better than having them lying in bed drinking beer."

Public opinion lay somewhere between the prime minister's view of a leisure society and the public service view of beer-drinking idlers. Polled the previous year, a substantial majority of Canadians (68 percent) believed the government was not strict enough in checking UI claimants.

In 1978 unemployment was still high at 8.2 percent. There were few left who thought the economic crisis was restricted to

Canada. Still, the introduction of tougher UI legislation was justified by the need to reduce disincentives to work and to "encourage workers to establish more stable work patterns and longer attachments to the active workforce." To this end, benefits were reduced from 66 percent of earnings to 60 percent, and the 12-week qualifying period was increased to 20 weeks for new entrants to the workforce. But tougher UI regulations based on implied malingering by workers failed to make the desired impact on public opinion. By 1982 over 39 percent of Canadians polled gave world economic pressures as the main cause of unemployment compared to 12 percent who believed the cause was people not wanting to work. In fact, these percentages were a complete reversal of those of 1977 when 29 percent believed the cause of unemployment was people not wanting to work, while 24 percent chose world economic pressures. The "malingering and fraud" theory still needed some selling.

Over the next 10 years the government stepped up its administrative measures to detect abuse of unemployment insurance. A new Report on Hirings system was introduced which gathered information from employers on new hirings, allowing the Employment and Immigration Department to check on claimants who failed to report work and earnings. In addition, a new computerized post-audit program was intended to track down unreported earnings by using past employment records. Selective investigations were also undertaken for the purpose of detecting fraud. The Report on Hirings system, especially, was given extensive publicity.

At the end of the 1980s the required qualifying period was again increased, though unemployment was 9.5 percent. In regions with unemployment rates below 9.5 percent it could take 20 weeks to qualify compared to the 14 weeks required since the late 1970s when national unemployment was 7.2 percent. And further, according to Employment and Immigration Minister Barbara McDougall, the government proposed to strengthen considerably the penalties for "fraudulent use of the unemployment insurance program." The new cut-backs met with no objection from the media, nor was there any criticism of the government's preoccupation with fraud.

The 15-year campaign to lay the blame for unemployment on

the unemployed had finally worked. The public was convinced; the government had even convinced itself. Canadians were turning their attention to the federal deficit. Over 70 percent of those polled in 1989 expressed concern about the deficit. In fact, well over a third of Canadians thought a balanced budget should be a greater government priority than unemployment.

People on welfare were also suffering the slow death of a thousand cuts. As federal UI regulations tightened in the 1970s, more and more unemployed workers, no longer eligible or with benefits expired, were forced onto provincial and municipal welfare rolls. Historically welfare caseloads had been largely made up of individuals who were classified as unemployable — people with disabilities or in poor health, and single mothers with child care responsibilities. Caseloads took on a new look by the end of the 1970s with a dramatic increase in the number of employable applicants. Nearly everyone had heard of a Ph.D. or two on welfare. Still, the numbers kept rising and provincial welfare rate increases began to drag behind inflation. In discretionary areas of eligibility, welfare officials began to choose denial of benefits more often than they had in the past.

Food banks were created to make up the difference — they were to be temporary arrangements by voluntary organizations but soon became permanent fixtures in most communities. Provincial governments began to extol the virtues of private voluntary solutions to the problems of poverty, but the truth was that most users of food banks were in receipt of government welfare cheques which fell short of providing enough money for both rent and food. Some Canadians failed to make the connection between food banks and the reduced purchasing power of welfare cheques that were not indexed to inflation. Many who did make the connection actually preferred the return to food hand-outs rather than giving the poor the freedom to spend cash in the grocery story (with all the lack of trust that was historically implied in the distinction). Many reported a "feel good" dimension to donating to private charities like food banks, a dimension missing from payroll deductions for government social programs.

There were other developments that created a whole new population of welfare recipients and changed the face of Canadian cities with a general acceptance by the public that was almost frightening. Poor economic conditions continued, leading to a reduction in housing starts and competition for fewer and fewer vacancies. By the end of the 1970s the lower end of the housing market experienced an acute shortage. The disturbing sight of people sleeping in doorways and over heat vents became familiar in most urban centres. Society had no trouble finding a name for them — the homeless — but there was less success in finding them homes. Their ranks were swelled when institutions previously serving the psychiatrically disabled, the mentally challenged, the physically disabled, and those in the justice system began to close down in the interests of economic restraint and, even hopefully, the opportunity for more successful rehabilitation in the community. On the Prairies the reserve-to-city migration movement was also an important factor. Unfortunately there were few funds available to solve the problems of the poor and the new population thrown onto the streets. As a result, emergency shelters were transformed during the 1980s from temporary to permanent housing solutions in Toronto, Montreal, Vancouver, Edmonton, Winnipeg, Regina, and many other cities.

Through to the end of the 1980s, however, welfare recipients generally were spared the public's wrath. Provincial governments which were responsible for welfare spending blamed the soaring welfare rolls on poor economic conditions and less access to UI benefits, both of which they attributed to federal policies. This rationale seemed to satisfy the general public, although it would not be sustained in the 1990s.

•••

The 1974 increases in family allowances were the last parents would receive before the program was gradually reduced and devalued over the next 15 years. Only three years later the government was under attack in the House of Commons for public statements by cabinet members that the family allowance for the first child might be eliminated. Also under consideration was a proposal to stop indexing allowances relative to the cost of living. Whether the government was serious about these proposals or just floating a trial balloon, as several members suggested, any intention of making changes was denied and the matter put to rest — but only temporarily.

Within a few months the prime minister indicated to an audience in southwestern Ontario that Canadians might see amendments to the universal family allowance program during the next Parliament. Once again the government denied that changes were being considered. In 1978 the denials stopped and the government announced a new direction that would shift funds from the family allowance program to a child tax credit. Family allowances were to be reduced by $8 a month for each child, while the child tax credit would rise by approximately $12. There was a great deal of rhetoric proclaiming that this new policy would still safeguard the universal aspect of the family allowance program but, in effect, part of existing funding was now moved to a non-universal program for children.

The government was clearly acting on a mixed message from the public. Canadians wanted universal social programs to remain universal. At the same time they did not intend "universal" to include high-income Canadians. Polls repeatedly phrased questions about family allowances as a choice between continuing payments to the well-to-do versus higher payments for those in need. Not surprisingly, Canadians opted for higher payments for those in need (65 percent in polls conducted throughout the 1970s). In this Hobson's choice, middle-income parents were forgotten and the bulk of their child benefits were income-tested from 1978 on.

After four years of reduced benefits, family allowances were de-indexed in 1982 as part of the government's so-called six-and-five strategy to combat inflation. It was clear that policymakers were beginning to feel confident about waning public support for family allowances. The head of the Canadian Council on Social Development, speaking to the standing committee on health, welfare and social affairs, insisted they were wrong:

> ....[A]ll these initiatives appear to be inspired by a perceived shift in public opinion, rather than by rational policy development. Of course, this is a very dangerous way to develop priorities since perceptions can be illusory.

In fact, most of the support for family allowances was coming from social agencies. The general public had lost interest.

The new Conservative government, taking office in 1984 and vowing to treat universal social programs as a "sacred trust," introduced an agenda that included control of government spending. Finance Minister Michael Wilson warned, "One of the key factors in the growth of government spending is automatic indexation of transfer programs to the consumer price index." When changes were protested in the House, the government reminded the opposition party of its own record of cut-backs and de-indexation. In the same year the public outcry about de-indexing of old age pensions forced the government to withdraw its policy with regard to pensions, but the de-indexing of family allowances remained in effect. The family allowance program was dying a slow death.

By the end of the 1980s the universality of family allowances had given its last gasp. Tax-backs for high-income Canadians, the now well-known "claw-backs," were introduced and, despite vigorous debate in the House, there was little public interest.

•••

During the same period the national health care system was also threatened. When price and income ceilings were lifted in the late 1970s the provincial practice of imposing hospital user fees and the medical profession's practice of extra-billing were greatly expanded in many provinces. In addition, there was a public perception that the 1977 federal-provincial financing arrangements, which began to use block funding rather than 50-50 cost-sharing, had allowed the provinces to divert health funds for other purposes. With general public concern about the risk of national health care becoming a two-tier system and more specific pressure from a newly formed Health Coalition, the government appointed a review commission headed by former Supreme Court Justice Emmett Hall. Its assignment was to look into charges that federal health funds were being diverted by the provinces and that extra-billing and user fees were violating access to the health care system. The announcement of the review was supported across the country, especially its mandate to look into extra charges. As the *Globe and Mail* commented briefly:

"Most Canadians want universal health insurance."

After a year of study the Hall inquiry found no evidence that provincial governments were using federal funds for non-health purposes. It did take seriously, however, the challenge to the health care system of extra charges to patients. It concluded:

> If extra-billing is permitted as a right and practised by physicians in their sole discretion, it will, over the years, destroy the program, creating in that downward path a two-tier system incompatible with the societal level which Canadians have attained.

Given the history of Canadian medicare, the reaction of the medical profession should have come as no surprise. The president of the Ontario Medical Association immediately responded with a threat that a ban on extra-billing could prompt strike action by some of its members. Control over doctors' fees, he warned, would turn doctors into civil servants working for the government, not for their patients. The executive director of the B.C. Medical Association called the Hall report a socialist document and added: "I can see down the road some unpleasant confrontations." The president of the Alberta Medical Association contended that forcing doctors to practice without allowing extra-billing would be a form of conscription and would give Canada a medicare system even more socialized than Britain's. The president of the Canadian Medical Association was certain that doctors would unionize if the recommendations were implemented. The Hall proposals were "not in the best interest of the public or the profession." These arguments and variations on the same theme were publicly echoed by doctors and their associations over the next year.

Following the Hall findings, a task force on federal-provincial financing held further meetings across the country and recommended that the two health acts (hospital insurance and medicare) be consolidated into one piece of legislation. The key to the new act would be the requirement of explicit criteria to be met by the provinces before federal funding would be granted. It was a clear threat to the autonomy the provinces had fought for over the past 20 years. Not surprisingly they rejected the task force proposals and the debate simmered for another two years, during which the federal minister of health and welfare, Monique Bégin, was highly visible and vocal but failed to bring in the recommended legislation (by then known as the Canada Health Act). In the meantime federal grants to the provinces for medicare and hospital insurance were cut back as part of the government's restraint program. The reductions were like a red flag waved at a bull. Provinces began to retaliate by re-introducing user fees. In 1983, when Alberta took this step, the federal health minister saw it as provocative and warned the provincial health minister that Alberta would lose up to $20 million a month in federal cash payments for every month user fees were in effect. Alberta responded that it would go to court to defend its right to set the fees, and added: "We hope our action will encourage others to join the battle, if necessary." B.C. followed with increases to its user fees within four months.

Against this background the Canada Health Act was introduced by the end of the year when polls showed almost 80 percent of Canadians were against extra-billing and user fees. After two months of committee hearings, it was debated in the House for less than four days before it was passed unanimously.

Throughout the rest of the 1980s the national health care program suffered along with other social programs as the federal government began to attack the deficit in earnest. But reductions in federal payments to the provinces for health insurance and medicare received little protest. Canadians who had fought so hard for medicare during the extra-billing crisis now agreed with the government that the deficit was more important than the current level of services. There was a brief surge of renewed support, even indignation, when American negotiators threatened to put Canada's social programs on the table during free trade talks in the late 1980s. Canadians may have been willing to let their own government put a balanced budget ahead of medicare, but they cried foul when the U.S. government suggested it might be a negotiable subsidy.

•••

While unemployment insurance, family allowances, and health care were subjected to cut-backs and erosion of universality during the

1970s and 1980s, the Canada Pension Plan ran into difficulties of another kind. In the mid-1970s public pressure, especially from organized labour, began to focus on the low level of CPP benefits. The fact that the CPP paid to average Canadians only 25 percent of the annual income of their working years placed Canada among the lowest of Western democracies in the adequacy of its national pension. The federal government responded to the growing pressure with promises of "pension reform."

It became clear, however, that the intention was to encourage the reform of private-sector pensions — by increasing labour force coverage, indexing benefits, making plans portable, and improving benefits for women — leaving the CPP as a lower layer of pension coverage on which more adequate layers could be provided by the private pension industry. To this end, the federal government set up a Senate committee in 1979, followed by a task force in 1980, to look into the pension situation in Canada, both public and private. Throughout these studies the threat of expanding the CPP was dangled before the private sector. A Vancouver speech by Health and Welfare Minister Bégin was typical. She warned that, if improvements in private pensions were too long in coming, "we would have to consider very strongly the possibility of taking action in the public sector."

The private sector, however, refused to be pushed into making what it considered costly changes. Neither would it support any expansion of the CPP. The general public, made up of workers who would benefit from CPP increases, watched with frustration and confusion as the pension debate between public and private sectors heated up in the media.

Canadian business strongly supported private pension plans and opposed CPP expansion, but its position had nothing to do with what was best for the elderly. The real reason was soon made clear in presentations to government-appointed committees and task forces. The introduction of the CPP in 1963 had thrown a scare into insurance companies and others in the pension industry, but far from showing any decline, pension funds had grown dramatically over the next 10 years. In 1965 private pension fund assets in Canada totalled $9 billion; by 1979 they reached $55 billion. In that year an estimated $35 billion in pension funds were invested in the Canadian private sector. Pension funds were, in fact, the largest source of investment capital in Canada.

Investments by pension funds ranged from conventional portfolio investment to direct ownership — acquisition of properties in the petroleum industry, oil and gas exploration and production, and large urban real estate projects were a few examples.

In light of these developments, the Canadian Manufacturers' Association argued that expansion of the CPP would be at the expense of private pensions and would deprive industry of a massive pool of funds needed to raise productivity and create jobs. The *Financial Post* agreed, commenting:

Pension funds are properly expected to play a large role in helping to fill this decade's huge capital requirements, especially in the energy sector.

The *Globe and Mail* argued that the investment of CPP funds by the provinces was a poor substitute. "The money is invested in nonproductive provincial assets, sometimes carelessly," an editorial claimed. "The private sector, on the other hand, can invest pension money in productive ventures."

Besides presenting its case at government hearings, business organized itself into a pressure group[9] for further action on other fronts. *Pensions and Survival*, a book commissioned by the group, warned that CPP expansion would have serious consequences. An aging population would place an undue burden on the workforce in the future as the ratio of pensioners to workers increased. Partially funded plans like the CPP left too much funding to future generations. Newspapers and periodicals took up this prophecy of doom. They painted pictures of drastically reduced paycheques for workers whose tax deductions would go straight to unproductive elderly Canadians. It was only a hint of the stirring up of intergenerational resentment that would reach a much more substantial level in the 1990s.

The government's long-awaited pension reform was finally unveiled in 1984. No changes to CPP benefit levels were recommended, an indication that the government took seriously the alarm raised by the business community. With the door closed on CPP increases, elderly Canadians without private pensions would continue to live on the basic payments provided by the wage-related Canada Pension Plan, the universal Old Age Security, and the means-tested Guaranteed Income Supplement. As a result, well over half of single Canadians over 65 lived in poverty.

The following year, a new government dealt another blow. Control of government spending, announced in the finance minister's spring budget, was to include the de-indexation of old age security pensions. This was the same minister and the same spending control referred to earlier in the de-indexation of family allowances. Though the family allowances legislation went ahead and was enacted with relative ease, in the case of old age pensions the government ran into stiff opposition. Senior citizens, with considerable help from opposition parties, bombarded members of Parliament with protest mail, staged rallies on Parliament Hill, and personally confronted the prime minister as he stepped from his limousine. Within a week of the budget presentation, the finance minister began to talk about a short-term trial period for de-indexing, after which the government would certainly review its decision. Within two more weeks the Canadian Chamber of Commerce, the Business Council on National Issues, and the Canadian Organization of Small Business joined in the outcry against the de-indexing proposal. The following day headlines announced: GOVERNMENT BACK-PEDALS ON PENSIONS.

As many seniors feared, it was only a temporary victory in the battle to keep old age security intact. The introduction of "clawbacks" followed in 1989. Most Canadians, however, were by then in favour of paying old age pensions only to the needy, and no campaign was mounted to maintain universality which had turned out to be not so sacred after all.

Fifteen years of watching social programs being cut back and de-indexed had failed to ruffle the feathers of most Canadians. Spending had to be controlled, and perhaps it was now too costly to care about each other. But however uncaring Canadians were at the end of the 1980s, they would become even more so as the 1990s unfolded.

CHAPTER 9

The End of Compassion

Canadians could have headed into the last decade of the century with a feeling of accomplishment and pride. Instead they were overcome with discontent, ill will, and much looking back in anger. How could past generations have been so irresponsible as to use public funds to help the unemployed, the sick, the young, and the elderly? What could have possessed them to care about their neighbours and even strangers in other parts of the country, leaving their children and grandchildren with a huge debt they may not be willing to pay?

This general malaise most certainly had its origin in poor economic conditions which included high interest rates, new taxes, stagnant incomes, and an unemployment rate of over 11 percent in the early 1990s.[10] The perception of most Canadians, rightly or wrongly, was that if you weren't out of a job, you soon would be. But by some twist of logic, the federal deficit, not unemployment, became the No. 1 concern of Canadians — a government saddled with a deficit was in no position to contribute to business recovery. Or so Canadians were told again and again. At every income level anxiety about our unbalanced budget spread. At the end of the 1980s, polls had shown, approximately 71 percent of Canadians were concerned about the deficit; by 1994 the proportion of people concerned had risen to 83 percent. Even more specifically, 70 percent of Canadians, who were asked if the federal government should increase spending to stimulate the economy or cut spending to reduce the deficit, replied that spending should be cut.

Concern about the deficit soon became anger as the public looked around for someone or something to blame. The culprits were not hard to find. Two items that everyone could understand jumped out of the federal budget: social programs (despite studies that attributed very little share of the deficit to social spending) and the national debt. They were not just impersonal lines on a budget page. They represented real people, real Canadians who were somehow responsible for the mess that Canada had become, a country rated by the United Nations year after year as the best place in the world to live (based on a measure of achievements in health, knowledge, and standard of living), but a country still dependent on the credit rating of Moody's Investment Services in the U.S., the *fourth* best place to live, in order to borrow on the international money markets.

One group targeted was a whole generation, those to blame for the national debt, Canadians between 45 and 65 years of age who irresponsibly encouraged the government to spend more and tax less during the 1970s and 1980s. Conceivably this generation should have been more aggressive in turning back the welfare state programs of the postwar period (though there were plenty of cuts as we have seen). Because they chose instead to continue payments to less fortunate Canadians they were strongly resented in the 1990s for their negligence, if not immorality.

Their critics were under-40 Canadians who, as the 1990s plodded on through difficult times, became more and more angry at the bad hand they had been dealt. Jason Ford, a University of British Columbia student who led a new organization called the Youth Alliance for Debt Freedom, was perhaps younger than most critics, but his press statement would have made any parent proud:

> Canada's youth are second-class citizens whose futures have been mortgaged to pay for services which their parents have long ago used up. It is not at all surprising that my parents and the parents of other Canadians my age should desire to have a high standard of living. What is disgusting is that all of them apparently expect their children to pay for what they have bought...It is pathetic and immoral for them to treat their sons and daughters as wellsprings of

cash. They have lived for too long on credit, hoping their children would pay it all back.

Middle-aged and near-middle-aged objects of such attacks either went into hiding or publicly admitted the folly of their past actions. The *Globe and Mail's* Jeffrey Simpson was one of the latter, admitting his generation "had been the least responsible and most selfish in the peacetime history of Canada." And since one of the largest appropriations his generation had made for itself during the good years was pensions, it had therefore "borrowed not only for its current needs but for its future retirement." Given this legacy, younger Canadians might properly "demand a settling of accounts," according to Simpson, by revoking some of the benefits the previous generation had provided for itself with the next generation's money. It was clear the public outcry about Canada's debt had become so general that even those responsible for it were afraid to be out of step.

Though the national debt created some intergenerational hostility, people who received benefits from social programs incurred most of the wrath of Canadians looking for someone to blame for the deficit. The unemployed were the main target, the elderly to a lesser degree. Since the unemployed made up 11 percent of the workforce and the elderly made up 15 percent of the adult population, roughly three-quarters of Canadians were feeling some resentment toward the remaining quarter (assuming, of course, that children were not mad at anyone). It was not the best of times.

Former federal cabinet adviser Dalton Camp lamented this new philosophy that compassion was no longer affordable. He noted:

> ....[I]n the present unsettled economic condition, voters have changed identities, seeing themselves less as citizens of compassion and caring and more as taxpayers. Their governments, alert to wind-shifts as any mariner would be, have cheerfully supported the taxpayers in their demands for restraint and fiscal responsibility.

The general acceptance of unemployment insurance restraint was a good example. With unemployment at 11.3 percent in 1992, the federal government response was to announce its latest success in tracking down fraud with technology acquired in the 1980s. Overpayments "of questionable motive" typically resulted from unreported work and earnings. New groups were the targets of its investigative work — self-employed people and full-time students, both areas of known UI fraud, the government claimed. Though overpayments had dropped slightly in recent years, officials claimed the decrease did not necessarily mean there was less abuse. Canadians could rest assured the Employment and Immigration Department would stay on the trail of UI cheaters. By inference, most of the unemployed were not really unemployed despite Statistics Canada figures to the contrary but, when asked the extent of overpayments, officials revealed they represented only 1.3 percent of total benefits paid.

The preoccupation of the Employment and Immigration Department with fraud was good news to Canadians who were lucky enough to have jobs and who were not entirely convinced that those without jobs deserved much sympathy. An Environics poll showed a fairly strong belief among Canadians that cheating by social program recipients was widespread and that social assistance programs, in particular, discouraged self-sufficiency.

This popular view was reinforced during the same year when the chairman of the House of Commons finance committee called for a 25-percent reduction in UI benefits. Claiming UI cheques were so generous they encouraged people to turn down jobs, he deplored the poor work ethic of many Canadians. "It's time to get people off the Lotto 10-40 Program and put them on the Prosperity Program," he said in an *Edmonton Journal* interview.

Later in the year the government did introduce UI changes, reducing all benefits and completely disqualifying those who quit their jobs without just cause. Challenged about the reduction in benefits when unemployment was so high, Employment Minister Bernard Valcourt urged the 1.6 million unemployed Canadians to be proud they were able to help pay off Canada's debts by taking lower payments. He turned a deaf ear to demands to reconsider the disqualification of workers who quit their jobs. Such workers deserved to be cut off, he said. In full support was Finance Minister Don Mazankowski who added that the government would not pander to "bleeding hearts" by spending more and more on social programs without regard for the deficit.

On the other hand, a business liaison group felt UI cuts had not gone far enough. The group, which included the Canadian Bankers Association, the Canadian Federation of Independent Business and the Canadian Chamber of Commerce, pressed the government the following year to pare down unemployment insurance even further by increasing entrance requirements to 20 weeks and requiring two weeks of work to earn one week of benefits.

Further cut-backs to unemployment insurance, longer qualifying periods, and reduced benefits to frequent users were brought in by the government in 1995. An Angus Reid poll found 73 percent of Canadians in support of the new changes compared to 22 percent who opposed. The most frequently offered reason for support was the belief that the changes would stop abuse of the system. And despite an unemployment rate of 9.5 percent, over 74 percent of those polled believed Canadians needed to take more responsibility for their own job security. These findings, according to the pollsters, showed the strong attachment of Canadians to the value of work.

People on welfare were also in for a hard time from the public. And increasingly the jobless ended up on welfare as UI benefits ran out under stricter regulations. In 1992 over 42 percent of those officially unemployed were no longer covered by unemployment insurance.

At first negative public attitudes resurfaced about the spending habits of people on welfare. The belief that allowances were being wasted was widespread, reminiscent of the 1920s when public relief was first distributed. An *Ottawa Citizen* editor, for example, argued that Ontario welfare regulations were based on the false premise that all poor were equally deserving of help while the reality was that many welfare recipients squandered their monthly benefits. He added:

In this woolly welfare world a ne'er-do-well spendthrift who wasted the last year drinking and gambling away a fortune in Las Vegas has just as much right to scarce provincial welfare funds as a 20-year veteran of the assembly line thrown out of work by the free trade agreement.

A *Toronto Star* columnist deplored what he saw as "the glorification of ineptness" when advocates complained that welfare recipients, unable to stretch their meager allowances, had to make regular trips to the food bank. In the same city on the same day a welfare worker listed the following examples of wasteful spending by young mothers on welfare — buying Pampers diapers, using throwaway inserts for baby bottles, feeding the baby name-brand food, and keeping the baby on baby food long after it was necessary, all for the mother's convenience.

These were not isolated attitudes. A Decima research poll conducted in 1993 found Canadians in a sour mood about social assistance, believing that many who received welfare were not truly in need. Interviewers reported a relatively strong sense that welfare recipients wasted their allowances.

And century-old arguments began to reappear that the absence of jobs was not the problem — people on welfare in Canada were simply lazy. A sweatshirt in a Vancouver store window carried a message that was growing in popularity: KEEP WORKING! MILLIONS ON WELFARE DEPEND ON YOU! With the unemployment rate at a nine-year high of 11.6 percent, a reader commented ruefully in a letter to the *Vancouver Sun*: "You might think that when the chips are down, everyone would be more generous."

Across the country people on welfare were also attacked on another front in the 1990s. In Metro Toronto, as officials watched welfare costs soar, they began to spread the word that many welfare recipients were cheating the system. A welfare hotline (quickly dubbed the "snitch line") was set up to allow other Torontonians to report those suspected of cheating. People couldn't get to their telephones fast enough — on the first day of operation 250 calls were taken. The nearby municipality of Durham was also concerned about its rising welfare costs. Without Toronto's resources, Durham Council had to forego a snitch line and instead asked its own council members to report fellow citizens they suspected were abusing the welfare program.

In Toronto the calls continued to pour into the snitch line. Torontonians also wrote to newspaper editors. A typical letter writer complained:

Anyone who hasn't recently been hatched knows what a sham some low-lifes make of the system...The wimpy politicians who make our laws aren't going to be tough on these thieves.

Montreal Gazette columnist Wayne Grigsby, visiting Toronto in the midst of the welfare-cheat furore, was struck by the "general snippishness in the air." He wrote:

Torontonians are a cranky lot this week, despite early and tantalizing sputterings of spring... An Environics poll made public this week suggests 34 percent of Torontonians think welfare benefits are too high, as opposed to 14 percent who think benefits are too low... Fifty-two percent feel some recipients fiddle the system, while a significant 20 percent feel it's something most or all welfare recipients do.

When Metro Toronto finally received a breakdown of the snitch line calls, the results were disappointing. The majority of calls were unfounded, said an internal report. The department head admitted allegations of fraud were "blown right out of proportion." The *Toronto Star* reported details of the findings. Of 780 calls received:

....[I]nvestigators found evidence of intent to defraud the system in three cases...These three cases have cost taxpayers an estimated $9,334, while an estimated $21,588 in overpayments were going to people without their knowledge because of administrative errors.

This breakdown of overpayments was typical of welfare investigation findings in most jurisdictions over the years. Historically more overpayments were due to errors made by welfare staff than were due to misrepresentation by clients. But Toronto citizens were not the only ones whose accusations flew in the face of the facts. During the same period welfare fraud was also being investigated in Ottawa. Though past studies in Ottawa had also shown the majority of overpayments were the result of administrative errors, the investigation went ahead with considerable public support. When completed it uncovered fraud costs representing only one percent of the welfare budget.

Despite these findings in both cities, welfare abuse rumours in Ontario refused to go away. There were also welfare cases at the provincial level (generally single mothers and people with disabilities), and a month later the provincial social services minister announced the government's intention of cracking down on fraud among these recipients.

Anxiety about welfare fraud spread like a virus across the country. In B.C. the government began working with the RCMP to tighten up on those defrauding the system. When the opposition party became impatient and called for a royal commission, the government responded by hiring 200 additional staff and reviewing new requirements for welfare applicants, such as photo identification and fingerprinting. In Quebec (home of Wayne Grigsby who had detected a collective mean spirit in Toronto a month or two earlier), the income security minister upgraded a number of welfare inspectors in response to public pressure about fraud. Their new status gave them additional power to get financial information from banks and ask neighbours, landlords, or employees at the corner store about the living arrangements of welfare recipients under suspicion. In Nova Scotia the health and welfare minister promised critics that abuses would be investigated.

It was contagious. An overly enthusiastic official of the federal Immigration Department reported that Somali refugees were ripping off Canada's welfare system and sending money back home to warlords. According to the *Toronto Star*, the leaked report claimed an estimated 91 percent of Somalis were on welfare. Their applications, said the report, were part of a plan by Somali clan leaders who had arranged the mass export of refugees to Canada with the sole purpose of sending welfare cheques back home. It was a made-to-order story for a public ready to believe the worst about both welfare recipients and immigrants. Ontario's opposition leader tapped these feelings, using the story to challenge the government about its social assistance budget. In the end, however, the report was disowned by the federal immigration minister, Sergio Marchi. The conclusions were not supported by the facts, he contended.

"Unfortunately the public has come to believe that a large percentage of refugee claimants are engaged in some type of fraudulent activity," he said. "This is simply not the case."

For Canadians who believed welfare recipients were wasteful, lazy, and dishonest, the idea of making them work for their payments had considerable appeal. In February 1993, the city of Thunder Bay, Ontario declared its intention to be the first in the province to make welfare recipients work for their welfare cheques. In May Alberta's social services minister announced that welfare employables would be put to work maintaining parks and seniors' residences or cleaning up rivers and highways. In August 700 mayors in Quebec agreed that 820,000 Quebecers who received unemployment insurance or welfare would soon be forced to do unpaid community work. All these initiatives were known familiarly as workfare, totally unacceptable in the past to most provinces and municipalities on moral grounds and, in fact, unacceptable to the federal government under terms of the Canada Assistance Plan.

Support for workfare had actually been growing for some time. Earlier in the year the federal government, working with focus groups, had found participants generally supportive of making people work for their welfare benefits. The study found that, not only were the focus groups in favour of workfare, but "the appeal for the idea seemed to stem from a sense of its punitive aspects."

It was a whole new philosophy for Canadians. A few rejected it. The *Globe and Mail's* Michael Valpy commented:

> Gone, vanished, are the concepts of social assistance as part of the Canadian ethic of a collective, mutually supportive society, of the Canadian ethic of a willingness to provide — as a right — a decent level of support for those citizens fallen upon hard times.

The worst was yet to come for those on welfare. In the fall of 1993 the Alberta government reduced welfare benefits by $26 a month and lowered rent allowances by up to $100 with the support of the vast majority of Albertans. The public's lack of sympathy was not a new attitude, according to an *Edmonton Journal* article. Editorial writer Linda Goyette commented:

The citizens of this province hate poor people…They can't think of a punishment too severe, a humiliation too deep, for people on welfare…The employed sit in judgment like small gods, squinting at the unemployed, asking: Are they deserving or undeserving? If these people can't pull themselves up by the bootstraps, well by damn, we'll give them a good, swift boot where it hurts.

But harsh measures for welfare clients were not confined to Alberta. Two years later Ontario residents cheered on a new government also intent on reducing welfare spending. Allowances were cut by over 21 percent for an estimated 1.3 million people on welfare. Leaner-and-meaner was followed within a year by meaner-and-meaner. Ontario announced a new workfare program which would require welfare recipients to earn their allowances by doing supervised community work. Other options such as training and job search (through an approved broker) received less publicity, but the main thrust of the announcement — workfare — was intended to satisfy a tough-minded public which, over a period of 10 years, had lost all compassion for people on public assistance.

A year later the Ontario public had further reason to celebrate — new welfare reforms entrenched the workfare program in legislation and extended it to single parents, introduced stricter measures to combat fraud including mandatory use of fingerprinting, allowed the government to place a lien on private homes, and threatened to make direct rent payments to landlords if welfare recipients failed to manage their allowances successfully. Those in the general public who saw nothing to celebrate in these changes simply looked the other way.

As each year of the 1990s failed to bring better economic times, an aging population gave non-elderly Canadians another source of irritation and pique.

The Canada Pension Plan was already beginning to show the strain, said some experts. A growing proportion of Canadians received benefits while the ratio of working people supporting pensioners grew smaller. The serious underfunding of the plan could eventually result in an underclass of impoverished senior citizens in the future, said other experts — not like today's seniors who were depicted as fit, well-to-do Canadians who crowded the golf courses of Florida or the ski hills of Quebec and B.C. Canadians were warned that the CPP benefits currently received by these fit seniors, in combination with current and past low contributions, would require contributions to go as high as 14 percent of earnings in less than 30 years. Solutions proposed by actuaries were to increase the retirement age and reduce survivors' benefits. These solutions were not likely to find their way into government policies, according to the *Vancouver Sun*. "Whenever governments anywhere in Canada make any proposals that affect pension incomes," an editorial pointed out, "seniors raise holy hell."

The truth was that seniors were not so successfully "raising holy hell" in the 1990s. Although 64 percent of Canadians still approved of the universality of old age security (OAS) in 1990, support began to dwindle over the next few years. *Vancouver Sun* columnist Barbara Yaffe wrote:

> Think about it. As things stand now, the single mom with a job, two kids and a ceiling-high pile of laundry to do this week has to kick in to help pay OAS for the likes of Pierre Trudeau, a millionaire receiving a trough-style pension who certainly could get by without the federal stipend.

This, of course, was inaccurate since the introduction of "clawback" legislation in the late 1980s, but the message was clear that further inroads on the universality of OAS would be welcomed by middle-income earners.

Pension discussions, like discussions about the national debt, often brought out intergenerational hostility that left one wondering whether family get-togethers across the country were nothing but free-for-alls. Pensioners were not the only target. Canadians about to retire in the next few years, those currently in their late fifties and early sixties, were anything but needy, according to a University of Toronto demographer who described them as the richest group in society. Attending a pension conference in Banff, he questioned why this group should receive CPP and other pensions and warned:

I can tell you that when my students do eventually get jobs they are not about to pay the benefits down the road for people who have had a 20-times better life than they can ever hope to have.

The media was also not above sowing a few seeds of discord. "Seniors Major Drain on Treasury" proclaimed a 1994 headline in the *Montreal Gazette*. Similar headlines became more frequent during the 1990s. The figures provided under such headlines failed to support the striking message, but unfortunately for seniors few bothered to read the detail. Quoting a federal Finance Department breakdown, the *Gazette* reported that seniors received $19 billion in federal payments the previous year, or 12 percent of total federal spending of $162 billion, not such an earth-shattering portion for 12 percent of the Canadian population.

Canadians were also concerned that the growing number of elderly would put more and more strain on the health care system. The elderly who get confused, misuse prescriptions, and end up in the doctor's office at public cost were, of course, only doing such things when they were not busy on the golf course or the ski hill. Even keeping the elderly alive is costly, said a Statistics Canada report. It warned that the increasing number of elderly would inevitably result in considerably higher health care spending as the weapons to fight death became more sophisticated. As a result, the StatsCan report went on, there may be new challenges to the traditional medical concept of "sustaining life at all costs." Presumably that would also include the lives of elderly ailing statisticians.

But in the 1990s the real issue related to the health care system was the continuing pressure for user fees. As the Honourable Emmett Hall had cautioned in 1980, over the years user fees would destroy the program, creating a two-tier system "incompatible with the societal level which Canadians have attained." Perhaps, sadly, the societal level attained by Canadians up to 1980 had dropped considerably by the 1990s and a two-tier system was no longer incompatible.

In 1992 Senator Claude Castonguay, often called the father of Quebec medicare, recommended that the federal government ease up on enforcing the Canada Health Act and allow some types of user fees. User fees, he claimed, "would make consumers think twice about whether they need certain services." Two months later the chairman of Royal LePage used the company's annual meeting to promote the concept of fees for health services. "I don't think the government should pay my health coverage," he said, "if I can afford to pay for it myself." In August the Canadian Medical Association passed a resolution at its annual meeting to ask for a change to the Canada Health Act so that high-income earners could pay part of their health care.

It was only the beginning. Early the following year the government of Alberta announced it would press the federal health minister for Canada Health Act changes to allow provinces to charge user fees. Specifically Alberta wanted to charge its residents $5 every time they visited their doctors. In the spring a study appeared (authored by the executive director of the Fraser Institute) recommending that wealthy Canadians should be allowed to go to the head of hospital and doctor queues if they paid the full costs of treatment.

In June 1994, according to the *Toronto Star*, a University of Ottawa health economist speaking in Winnipeg stated that Canadians routinely abused and misused the health care system, and user fees would serve as a wake-up call. In 1995 the Canadian Medical Association, only after considerable debate, defeated a resolution that Canadians who so desired (or who could afford) should be allowed to buy private insurance for all their medical services.

These developments over six years gave a mixed message as to where public opinion was heading with regard to a two-tiered health care system. Polled in two consecutive years, Canadians responded with confusion and uncertainty. In 1995 approximately 49 percent were in favour of a two-tiered system in Canada compared to 46 percent opposed. In 1996 results were reversed with 44 percent in favour and 49 percent opposed. Health care was consistently rated by Canadians as the most valued of their social programs (94 percent of Canadians surveyed by a U.S. medical journal in 1992 ranked Canadian health care as good to excellent), but it was clear the idea of having one system for the poor and one system for all others was not unacceptable to many.

In fact, the 1990s were not good years for social programs.

Unemployment insurance introduced in 1941 no longer provided the help workers needed between jobs. Instead, increased qualifying periods and decreased benefit periods threw many onto welfare before they were back in the workforce. The welfare system returned to its roots in the relief programs of the 1920s and 1930s, untrusting, stigmatizing, and ungenerous. Family allowances which were first paid to Canadian parents in 1945 were finally discontinued in 1993. Old age pensions introduced in 1951 and 1965 became more and more unpopular with working Canadians of the 1990s (and were regularly threatened) as they denied the past contributions of a whole generation and resented anything more than subsistence incomes for the elderly. Universal health care brought in during the 1950s and 1960s was on shaky ground, about to lose its universality as middle- and upper-income Canadians began to lose interest in keeping the same level of service for all Canadians, rich or poor. Though certain groups had become entitled to these benefits under duly enacted legislation, their benefits were now called hand-outs and resented by a new kind of society. A *Toronto Star* columnist expressed a view that was not uncommon: "Yes, the age of entitlement seems to be in its last days. I hope you don't mind if I don't shed a tear."

•••

Ten years ago in a movie otherwise long forgotten comedian Jonathan Winters played the role of an American who regularly prescribed: "We've gotta kick a little butt around here." He was cantankerous, unfeeling, rude — and quite funny. To Canadians the role epitomized the American glorification of individualism and self-sufficiency. Today the character he portrayed could just as easily be a Canadian, and somehow it doesn't seem quite as funny.

As we approach the end of the twentieth century, we can take little pride in the way we have reordered our values. We have become inured to the homeless on every downtown street. If we put anything in their outstretched baseball caps, we have to joke to companions that we only give on Tuesdays and Thursdays. After all, it has become acceptable, even mandatory, to be tough. When the homeless overflow into the indoor shopping malls on some of Canada's bitter winter days, we complain that the Salvation Army mission should allow them to lie on their cots all day so we don't have to look at them. While we drive our $30,000 or $40,000 SUVs along the streets and highways, we feel the scenery could be improved if welfare recipients were forced to clean up the debris in the parks and along the roadside.

We blame unemployment on the unemployed, the aging population on the elderly, and the demand for health care on people who are so anxious to sit for hours in doctors' waiting rooms that they make appointments even when they don't need them. And since much of public opinion is formed by an inherent need to conform to the views and values of the majority, Canadians are won over daily to this way of thinking. We see nothing on the horizon to disturb our new value system. Governments will, after all, eventually do what we ask. And if this is the public's definition of a caring society, policies and legislation will be made to fit.

Endnotes

1   See Terry Copp, *The Anatomy of Poverty: The Condition of the Working Class in Montreal, 1897–1929*; J.S. Woodsworth, *My Neighbor — A Study of City Conditions, A Plea for Social Service*; A.F.J. Artibise, *Winnipeg: A Social History of Urban Growth, 1874–1914*.

2   A Royal Commission of Enquiry appointed in 1915 found conclusive evidence of a conspiracy to obtain election funds from "extras" in the contract for the construction of the Manitoba Legislative building. The contractor had been overpaid by almost a million dollars, and a good portion of the overpayment found its way to the president of the Provincial Conservative Association.

3   An exception was the creation in 1911 of the Nationalist party which originated in Quebec and had members in the federal house for six years.

4   There were naturally many in Quebec who were unhappy about the province's declining birth rate, which led many local newspapers to turn the argument on its head. Rather than encouraging an increase in the birth rate, *La Boussole* complained, for example, the proposed family allowance with its minimal benefits after the fourth child would actually have the negative effect of inviting French Canadians to limit the size of their families.

5   In this account of the origins of health care in Saskatchewan and the subsequent development of Canada's national health care system, Malcolm Taylor's *Health Insurance and Canadian Public Policy* has been a valuable source of chronology and information.

6   In 1949 a Canadian Institute of Public Opinion poll showed 82 percent of Canadians in favour of industrial pensions. A 1950 CIPO poll showed 62 percent of Canadians believed labour unions had been a "good thing" for Canada; by 1956 this figure had risen to 67 percent.

7   An expanded version of the story, based on personal interviews, is also given by Peter C. Newman in *The Distemper of Our Times* and by Richard Simeon in *Federal-Provincial Diplomacy: The Making of Recent Policy in Canada*.

8   In *Unemployment in History: Economic Thought and Public Policy*, John A. Garraty provides an in-depth discussion of the history and philosophy of unemployment.

9   Called the Canadian Pension Conference, its members included such Canadian companies as the Aluminum Company of Canada, the Bank of Montreal, Canada Packers, Canadian Industries Limited, Canadian National Railways, Domtar, Dupont of Canada, Inco, Noranda Mines, Shell Canada, and the Steel Company of Canada.

10 Canadians were also faced with other public policy issues such as the Free Trade Agreement, the North American Free Trade Agreement, the Meech Lake and Charlottetown accords, and the erosion of funding for post-secondary education, social housing, and other programs, all of which drained public energy and added to the general malaise.

Selected Bibliography

Books and Journals

Allen, Richard, *The Social Passion, Religion and Social Reform in Canada 1914–1928* (Toronto: University of Toronto Press, 1971).

Artibise, Alan F.J., *Winnipeg: A Social History of Urban Growth, 1874–1914* (Montreal: McGill-Queen's University Press, 1975).

Badgley, Robin and Samuel Wolfe, *Doctors' Strike* (Toronto: Macmillan of Canada, 1967).

Calvert, Geoffrey, *Pensions and Survival, The Coming Crisis of Money and Retirement* (Toronto: Maclean Hunter, 1977).

Canada, *Canada's National-Provincial Health Program for the 1980's* (Ottawa, 1980).

Canada, *House of Commons Debates* and *Sessional Papers* (Ottawa).

Canada, *Senate Debates* (Ottawa).

Canada, Royal Commission on the Status of Women, *Report* (Ottawa, 1970).

Carman, Francis, "Canadian Government Annuities," *Political Science Quarterly*, vol. 30, no. 3, September 1915.

Copp, Terry, *The Anatomy of Poverty: The Condition of the Working Class in Montreal, 1897–1929* (Toronto: McClelland and Stewart, 1974).

Curtis, Clarence H., "The Labour Unions' Campaign for Pensions," *Canadian Banker*, 57 (Spring 1950), p. 87.

Garraty, John A., *Unemployment in History: Economic Thought and Public Policy* (New York: Harper & Row Publishers, 1978).

Guest, Dennis, *Emergence of Social Security in Canada* (Vancouver: University of British Columbia Press, 1980).

Industrial Canada, October 1908, p. 228; April 1914, p. 1135.

Labour Gazette, November 1914; March 1915.

Lower, Arthur R.M., *Colony to Nation* (Toronto: Longmans Canada, 1946).

Lubove, Roy, *Struggle for Social Security 1900–1935* (Cambridge: Harvard University Press, 1968).

MacInnis, Grace, *J.S. Woodsworth, A Man to Remember* (Toronto: Macmillan, 1953).

McNaught, Kenneth, *A Prophet in Politics* (Toronto: University of Toronto Press, 1959).

Morton, W.L., *The Progressive Party in Canada* (Toronto: University of Toronto Press, 1967).

Pickersgill, J.W. and D.F. Forster, *The Mackenzie King Record* (Toronto: University of Toronto Press, 1968).

Sheils, G.K., "Retirement Pensions," *Industrial Canada* (June 1950).

Social Services Council of Canada, *Social Services Congress — March 3-5, 1914, Report of Proceedings*, 1914.

Taylor, Malcolm G., *Health Insurance and Canadian Public Policy* (Montreal and Kingston: McGill-Queen's University Press, 1978).

Woodsworth, J.S., *My Neighbor – A Study of City Conditions, A Plea for Social Service* (Toronto: Missionary Society of the Methodist Church, 1911).

Wright, Jack, "What's Best for Pensions?" *Canadian Business* (March 1950).

Newspapers

Calgary Herald

"Social Security Plan Merits General Favor," March 17, 1943, p. 5.

Edmonton Journal

"Soup Kitchens Opened," February 24, 1908, p. 2.

"Premier King's Astonishing Speech," April 7, 1930, p. 4.

"Unemployment Insurance Adopted," August 3, 1940, p. 4.

"Social Security Blueprint," March 17, 1943, p. 4.

"Are Family Allowances Coming?" October 5, 1943, p. 4.

"Pension Bill Passed," April 3, 1965, p. 4.

"MP's Suggestion to Trim UI Benefits," reprinted in *Montreal Gazette*, February 16, 1992, B3.

Goyette, Linda, "Alberta Slashes Welfare," reprinted in *Ottawa Citizen*, September 9, 1993, A12.

Financial Post

"Baby Bonus Doubts," reprinted in *Montreal Gazette*, July 17, 1944, p. 8.

"Here's Why Labor Changed Its Strategy on Pensions," March 25, 1950, p. 3.

"Private Pension Plans Should Get Priority," April 18, 1981, p. 7.

Halifax Chronicle

"This Week in Ottawa," April 9, 1930, p. 6.

"Tariff and Reforms," January 5, 1935, p. 10.

"The Well Being of Our Children," June 23, 1944, p. 8.

"Baby Bonuses, Wages and Taxes," July 21, 1944, p. 8.

"Turning Point," March 31, 1965, p. 4.

Manitoba Free Press

"Modern Philanthropy," March 14, 1908, p. 11.

"Women of the Province are Given the Vote," January 28, 1916, p. 1.

"Problems Must be Faced," January 29, 1916, p. 15.

"The Problem of Unemployment," January 29, 1930, p. 15.

Montreal Gazette

"A Week at Ottawa," February 25, 1907, p. 9.

"Old Age Pensions," March 2, 1907, p. 8.

"Old Age Pension Bill," April 19, 1926, p. 12.

"Gross Abuse of the Dole," September 12, 1930, p. 14.

"The Tariff Changes," September 17, 1930, p. 14.

"Under Two Flags," January 4, 1935, p. 10.

"Won't It Be Wonderful?" March 16, 1943, p. 8.

"Spending Our Way to What?" July 20, 1944, p. 8.

Grigsby, Wayne, "Torontonians Showing a Collective Mean Spirit," February 23, 1992, A5.

"Job Quitters Deserve UI Cuts, Ottawa Insists," December 4, 1992, A1.

"Report on Somalis Cheating Welfare Contains Some Mistakes, Minister Says," November 13, 1993, A12.

"Seniors Major Drain on Treasury," January 7, 1994, B1.

"Some Medical User Fees OK," February 8, 1992, A6.

Ottawa Citizen

"Old Age Pension," March 6, 1914, p. 14.

"It's Still Rationed Poverty," March 18, 1943, p. 26.

"Pension Funds Carry Clout," December 3, 1980, p. 37.

Ford Jason, "Don't Make Youth Pay," January 19, 1992, B1.

Calamai, Peter, "Welfare World's Fuzzy Thinking Leaves Loopholes for Abuse," June 15, 1992.

Regina Leader-Post

"Expect Ceiling on Allowances," January 28, 1944, p. 1.

Toronto Globe

"Old Age Pensions," March 2, 1907, p. 8.

"Workmen's Compensation," letter, January 3, 1914, p. 4.

"Canadian Lumbermen in Annual Gathering," February 4, 1914, p. 15.

"Province Prospers But Has Many Evils," February 25, 1914, p. 1.

"Voice of the People," letter, April 23, 1926, p. 8.

"The Unreformed Senate," June 24, 1926, p. 4.

"Government to Regulate Business; Days of Laissez-Faire are Ended," January 3, 1935, p. 1.

"Unemployment and Health Insurance, Minimum Wage, Limited Work Week," January 5, 1935, p. 1.

"The First Instalment," January 5, 1935, p. 6.

Toronto Globe and Mail

"State Spends What People Earn," March 19, 1943, p. 6.

"Why Child Allowances Now?" September 23, 1943, p. 6.

"Will Grants Help the Children?" June 24, 1944, p. 8.

"Martin Announces Committee," March 11, 1950, p. 3.

"Playing with Words and Taxes," October 27, 1951, p. 6.

"All Platformless Liberals Ask is Cast Vote for Uncle Louie," July 25, 1953, p. 4.

"Can This Be Leadership?" July 20, 1953, p. 6.

"LaMarsh Links Pension Plan Fate, Career," September 27, 1963, p. 1.

"Pension Plan at Last—But Questions Remain," March 31, 1965, p. 6.

"Restrict MD's Fees, Scrap Premiums, Ottawa Told," September 4, 1980, p. 1.

"End to Extra Billing is Called Conscription by Doctors," September 4, 1980, p. 10.

"Tough, Clear Road," April 4, 1981, p. 6.

"Bégin Says Hospital User Fees Could Cost Alberta Millions," March 30, 1983, p. 1.

Simpson, Jeffrey, "A Tough Future Bequeathed to the Most Selfish Generation in Our History," September 22, 1994, A26.

Valpy, Michael, "Enter the Era of Mandatory Workfare," June 13, 1996, A22.

Toronto Star

"Canada's Coming Problems," March 7, 1914, p. 8.

"Health Plan Assured if Provinces Cooperate," October 4, 1955, p. 6.

"Cut Welfare Universality, LePage Boss Urges," April 1, 1992, F3.

"Welfare Low-Lifes Abuse System," letter, April 16, 1992.

Camp, Dalton, "It's the Sacred Trust vs. the Bottom Line," April 19, 1992, B3.

"Welfare Abuse Not Widespread," April 19, 1992, A7.

"Be Proud to Take Cut in Payments," December 4, 1992, A15.

Jones, Frank, "Welfare Life is Tough but Food Banks No Answer," June 17, 1993.

Toronto Telegram

"No Use Moralizing," reprinted in *Vancouver Province*, July 15, 1931, p. 6.

Vancouver Province

"A Protective Measure," March 11, 1908.

"The Industrial Conference," September 15, 1919, p. 6.

"Taking it Seriously," September 18, 1919, p. 6.

"The Industrial Conference," September 19, 1919, p. 6.

"Beveridge Plan for Canada," March 16, 1943, p. 4.

"Pensions: Canada Takes the Lead," March 31, 1965, p. 4.

Vancouver Sun

Ford, Tom, "The Age of Government Handouts Seems to be Coming to an End. Good," March 21, 1992, B2.

"Changes Needed to Support Growing Ranks of Elderly, Report Says," April 8, 1993, A1.

"Finding a Scapegoat," letter, May 19, 1993, A15.

"Let's Stop Slandering Welfare Recipients," letter, July 29, 1993, A3.

"Pension-day Deposits, on Social Outing," December 9, 1993, B1.

Yaffe, Barbara, "Advice for Ottawa, Don't Mess With Seniors," February 12, 1994, B3.

Kane, Michael, "Pensions in Peril, Don't Expect Smooth Sailing into Sunset on CPP Lifeboat," June 27, 1994, D8.

Victoria Times

"That Blank Cheque," August 31, 1931, p. 4.

"Canada's Plans," March 17, 1943, p. 4.

"Measure for Family Allowances May Prove Political Liability," July 27, 1944, p. 3.

"A Promise Fulfilled," March 31, 1965, p. 4.

Winnipeg Free Press

"The Vagueness of Mr. Bennett," January 5, 1935, p. 17.

"Doctors Find Health Insurance Bill Sound," March 17, 1943, p. 1.

Index

Date Due